OVID'S HEROINES

OVID'S HEROINES

A VERSE TRANSLATION OF THE *HEROIDES*

by
Daryl Hine

Yale University Press

New Haven
London

Medea to Jason and *Oenone to Paris* have appeared in the
Paris Review.

Designed by Sylvia Steiner.
Set in Sabon type by Keystone Typesetting, Inc., Orwigsburg,
Pennsylvania.
Printed in the United States of America by BookCrafters, Inc.,
Chelsea, Michigan.

Library of Congress Cataloging-in-Publication Data
Ovid, 43 B.C.–17 or 18 A.D.
[Heroides. English]
Ovid's Heroines : a verse translation of the Heroides / by Daryl
Hine.
p.   cm.
ISBN 0-300-05093-3 (cloth). — ISBN 0-300-05094-1 (paper)
1. Epistolary poetry, Latin—Translations into English.   2. Love
poetry, Latin—Translations into English.   3. Mythology,
Greek—Poetry.   4. Love-letters—Poetry.   5. Women—Poetry.
I. Hine, Daryl.   II. Title.
PA6522.H4H56   1991
871'.01—dc20   91-12011 CIP

The paper in this book meets the guidelines for permanence and
durability of the Committee on Production Guidelines for Book
Longevity of the Council on Library Resources.

10   9   8   7   6   5   4   3   2   1

FOR ANNE

Anna soror, soror Anna, meae omnis conscia culpae.
Heroides VII 191

CONTENTS

Numerals in parentheses refer to the traditional, but hardly the original, order of the epistles.

PREFACE

Heroines in name only, the passive but vocal victims of Ovid's epistolary elegiacs might better, if less neatly, be termed women of the Heroic Age, grandes dames, or famous females. In lieu of an anachronistic feminism, they display, from Hypermnestra to Sappho, a wounded femininity, ambiguous because imagined by a man—and an avowedly heterosexual man at that. Never is the feminine mystique more cruelly traduced, indeed parodied, than in the singular instance of Sappho, the sole subject in this gallery to have left a self-portrait, less fragmentary in Ovid's first century than in our twentieth. For the rest, literature, primarily in Greek, supplies the long-suffering models on which the gorgeous Latin tropes are hung. At the same time the poet-ventriloquist's lips can be seen, stylistically, to move, so that the challenge to the mimic-translator is to catch behind or within the voice of each victim-heroine the inimitable Ovidian tone. Bantering, ironical, elaborate, and often epigrammatic, when these qualities ill become dramatic naturalism, the words of Oenone or Phaedra, Briseis or Hermione, are always audibly those of our worldly, ingenious Roman author. Ovid is like a scribe or public letter writer to whom these unfortunate, often abandoned women dictate their heartbroken complaints.

The unity, not to say monotony, of the *Heroides*, then, is twofold—one of tone and one of fictional situation. At the same time this single-mindedness of plot, if not always of character, lends itself to the verbal variations and rhetorical pyrotechnics that are Ovid's stock in trade. Most of the one-sided relationships delineated in these imaginary love letters present a sorry if biased picture of relations between the sexes. Even that rare phenomenon, reciprocated love (as in I, XI, XIII, XVII, and XIX), is subject to circumstance and doubt. When the outcome, as in the last letter in

the traditional order, promises the comedic resolution of mar-
riage, the conviction remains that "men were deceivers ever,"
heroes and demigods more deceptive than most. Yet if our hero-
ines are seldom heroic in the strenuous modern sense, neither are
they all victims or dupes. Hypermnestra earns her stellar status by
an act of heroism or bravado marred or enhanced, according to
one's point of view or period, by signal self-sacrifice. Penelope's
patience, no less heroic, will be rewarded by the return of her
errant mate—as will Helen's petulant impatience but not Hero's.
In all instances further correspondence is redundant and there will
be no reply. It is not faith but fate that fails Hero and Laodamia,
who are disappointed rather than deceived, whereas so many
heroines are both. Finally, half a dozen of these desperate women
know almost as well as the reader what they are going to do. The
ignorance of the rest sharpens the irony inherent in dramatic
monologue as in the epistolary novel. Delivered or not, letters and
speeches are equally precariously poised upon a point in time,
snapshots or still studio studies in contrast to the moving film of
tragedy or epic. While spectators may or may not know what is in
the next frame, the protagonist can hardly guess, unless she takes
her fate into her own hands. Several of the letters (II, IV, VII, IX, XI,
XV, XIX) are suicide notes, though their writers may be unaware of
the fact. All of them, in a postal system even more undependable
than our own, would be marked "return to sender."

   In the corpus of these dead letters three signed by men have
traditionally been included. The self-serving if unapologetic mis-
sives from Paris (XVI), Leander (XVIII), and Acontius (XX) are not
replies to the epistolary outbursts of Helen (XVII), Hero (XIX), and
Cydippe (XXI), which rather they precede and provoke. The duet
implicit in such an exchange interrupts the series of bravura col-
oratura arias that constitutes the recital program of the *Heroides*.
Moreover, these masculine letters are of strikingly dubious au-
thenticity and merit; in fact, all the epistles from XV on have been
doubted at one time or another. I have, however, included them,

as I have many suspect and bracketed lines of the text for the sake of completeness. We do not have so much of Ovid or antiquity that we can afford to throw any of it out on grounds of provenance, prudery, or philological prejudice. At the same time I have rearranged the traditional but arbitrary sequence preferred by the manuscripts (none earlier than the eleventh century A.D., and thus equidistant between the modern reader and the ancient author). I have followed that mythological chronology which until recently furnished a set of reference points, as in a constellated heaven, to oral legend and written literature alike. From Hypermnestra, daughter of the eponymous founder of the Grecian race, Danaus, to quasi-historical Sappho, via the camp followers of the Argonauts and the women's chorus of the Trojan conflict in the following mythical generation, these verse letters sketch the legendary prehistory of Greece from an ostensibly feminine point of view.

Perhaps by the unchanging essence of human nature all we mean is that we cannot conceive of other nations and ages except in our own guise. Historical costume drama seems a comparatively newfangled masquerade, and an already obsolescent one, now that *metteurs en scene* situate the classics in any era but that indicated by the script. Shakespeare and company less self-consciously put Timon and Coriolanus in doublet and hose. Beneath the Grecian names and myths of the *Heroides* we may discern the Roman matrons (for though some are unwed, none is virginal) of Ovid's time, 43 B.C. to A.D. 17. The circles in which he moved embraced that class which figured prominently and exclusively in such gossip columns of the day as Suetonius' *Lives of the Caesars*. These and their mythic, Hellenic antecedents afford Ovid's readership—or audience, since the ancients, as seen in the last two epistles here, were little given to solitary, silent reading—the arcane pleasures of allusions recognized, which a wider public might enjoy today in the ghosted love letters of such contemporary heroines as, say, Mrs. Simpson or Marilyn Monroe. One signal difference is that such effusions are no longer penned, even by the least trendy amanuenses, in verse. Yet although one may detect behind Laodamia or Helen the highborn phantoms of Octavia or Julia, the Roman *Heroides* are not quite *romans à clef*, constituting though they do a series of one-sided epistolary novels (two-sided in the case of the correspondence between Cydippe and Acontius, Hero and Leander, and Paris and Helen). None of the erotic elegists, Catullus, Tibullus, Propertius, and Ovid in the *Ars Amatoria* and *Remedia Amoris*, presented the woman's point of view, let alone in woman's words. Ovid's transposition from Greek to Latin is nothing to his translation of feminine suffering and sentiment, with which he, like Virgil, seems to have had unusual sympathy, into the public theater of mankind. For Ovid, at least in the *Heroides*, women were not the objects but the subjects of pity and affection.

Often dismissed as a mere facile versifier by those to whom facility and verse are a closed book, Ovid is—or was—a notoriously easy read. His lapidary verse comparatively easy to construe as well, is nonetheless tricky to translate. Verbal polish may too carelessly be mistaken for superficiality, and lambent wit for flippancy. The man who wrote a treatise on cosmetics (*Medicamina Faciei Femineae*) as well as an account of the Roman religious calendar (*Fasti*) could not always keep a straight face. The polished perfection Ovid sought and seldom failed to achieve can come to seem slapdash; his epithets sometimes seem to have been selected more for metrical than for semantic appositeness. If meter and syntax are Ovid's structural strengths—and he was a stricter and more regular metrician than his near contemporary, Virgil, whom no one has ever accused of jocularity—his poetic diction is rather a letdown. His words, always appropriate at least, seldom excite wonder. More like Racine's than Shakespeare's, his vocabulary is restricted, plain, straightforward, and common though never vulgar, a kind of basic Latin that, though the beginning student's comfort, may prove the opportunity or despair of the translator. Few classical authors can boast fewer *hapax legomena,* those unique readings that are the delight of scholars. His fondness for the stock epithet, however, recommended Ovid to the eighteenth century. Along with the invention of that linguistic straitjacket, the dictionary, the Age of Reason saw multiple editions of the *Heroides,* translated by such masters of platitude as Otway, Tate, Rhymer, Dryden, and Pope. Only the last two need give the modern translator a moment's pause, though the modern reader will find their diction almost as impenetrably archaic as Latin. The decorous slang of one era, like its customs and costumes, becomes the archaeology of another, and the most accomplished translations must be, if not superseded, at least updated. Any new version that, like those of Rhymer and Tate, reproduced the poverty and approximateness of Ovid's diction would be unreadably dull; therefore the present translator pleads guilty to having spiced these ladylike letters with the salt of neologism and the sauce of slang.

Although this preface offers inadequate scope for a course in comparative metrics, I must attempt to account for my use of the same verse form as my Augustan predecessors, all the more so as I have departed from their practice in such matters as diction and in my preference for translation and imitation over paraphrase. All form is its own justification, but it should also be justified by content; if the formal peculiarities of the original are inimitable in English, some counterpart can usually be contrived. Formidable as the challenge may seem, so as to have defeated most modern translators of verse before they start, the formal cannot be credibly rendered by, or reduced to, the formless. Hence some sketch of Latin prosody seems in order.

The meter of the *Heroides,* the second most common in Latin, is the elegiac couplet. It consists of two lines of unequal length. The first, the dactylic hexameter, derived ultimately from Homer, is the commonest line in Latin, as the so-called iambic pentameter is in English. Such sturdy and popular vehicles admit of the

greatest variation. The second line of the elegiac couplet is the
hemiepes, which consists of the first part of the preceding line,
repeated:

$$-\,\underset{\smile}{\cup}\,-\,\underset{\smile}{\cup}\,-\,\underset{\smile}{\cup}\,-\,\underset{\smile}{\cup}\,-\,\cup\,\cup\,-\,\cup$$
$$-\,\underset{\smile}{\cup}\,-\,\underset{\smile}{\cup}\,-\,-\,\cup\,\cup\,-\,\cup\,\cup\,-$$

The basis of quantitative meters, in which first Greek, and later
Latin, verse was composed, is the length not just of the vowel but
also of the syllable, a convention so strange to our ears as to seem
inaudible, inured as we are, or as we used to be, to the strong
stress rhythm of English. Something of the effect of the pattern, if
not of the means by which it was once achieved, may be seen and,
I hope, heard in the following elegiac couplet from "Penelope to
Ulysses" (*Heroides* I, 31–32) in my alternate, accentual version:

> Someone, explaining fierce combats on top of the newly
> laid table,
>   Paints all of Pergamum there, using a droplet of wine.

These lines attempt to reproduce strictly, if rather stiffly, the Latin:

> Ātque aliquīs positā mōnstrāt fera prōelia mēnsā
>   Pīngit et ēxiguō Pērgama tōta merō.

There are three ways by which elegiacs can be responsibly
rendered into English, leaving aside prose and free verse as fla-
grant misrepresentations in which all poetic effect is sacrificed to a
dubious sense. Accentual approximation of quantitative meter, as
above, suffers from the absence of that syllabic substitution which
gives flexibility to the Latin hexameter, since whereas in music one

---

* *Ovid's Epistles, translated by several hands* (London: Jacob Tonson,
1705). Several of these hands are those of John Dryden, Thomas Otway,
Nahum Tate, and Thomas Rhymer, among others now less well known.
Alexander Pope's polished but excessively free version of *Sappho to
Phaon* can be found on pp. 125–131 of his *Poetical Works* (London:
Oxford University Press, 1966).

long equals two shorts, one stressed does not equal two unstressed syllables. An inevitable monotony underlines the oddity of such stressful measures, which may be read as merely syllabic, the ear often failing to catch that which it is unused to. By far the most widespread academic imitation of the elegiac couplet nowadays is typographical: two lines of uneven length alternate, the second indented but with no metrical dimension or excuse—at best syllabic and at worst free. The trouble with this solution is that although it looks something like the couplet in question, it does not scan or sound like it, appealing to a visual and conceptual sensibility that has lost touch with the oral basis of verse. Where the weight and position of every syllable was Ovid's primary preoccupation, affording a subliminal pleasure to his readers ever since, there remains nothing but a flat, tuneless printout. My approach, in which I have followed the precedent of the classic translations of 1705,* rests upon the axiom that, whatever its constituents, the elegiac couplet is undeniably a couplet, that is a usually self-contained metrical—and often semantic—unit, generally symmetrical, intermediate between stichic and strophic verse. (That it is occasionally a triplet is a convention and doubtless a convenience of seventeenth- and eighteenth-century practice). Now the only true couplet in English is a rhymed couplet. Although the strictures of an inflected language inhibited Ovid from a systematic use of rhyme, he did experiment with it. Moreover, the structure of the elegiac couplet produces a sort of metrical homeoteleuton, or identical ending: the second half of the second line, like the last two feet of the first, always preserves the same pattern of long and short syllables in Latin or of stresses in English. After all, our native heroic couplet has seemed to me best suited to the *Heroides,* as in the following anglicization of the lines from "Penelope to Ulysses" cited above.

> On tabletops they draw the battle line
> And write the *Iliad* in a drop of wine.

Ovid tells us in his *Tristia* (IV. x. 57–58) that he had barely begun shaving at the time of his first public recitation (the ancient form of publication) of certain juvenile poems that are generally thought to have been these one-man masques. Is it any wonder if his brilliant maiden exercises should derive from the genre with which he was best acquainted? Redolent of scholastic exercises, however polished and precocious, they once provided, and perhaps somewhere still provide, the first hurdles for beginning Latinists. Private and literary, Roman education envisaged a preparation for public life, and it was Roman law that constituted the whole of civil business. We know, again from the *Tristia,* that Ovid himself was both an advocate and a magistrate. The legal profession was, apart from the army, the only possible one for a gentleman, and only gentlemen were educated. Much of the future advocates' time was spent in mock debates, declamation, or *suasoria,* wherein a hypothetical case, usually weak (or worse), must be presented in the most pathetic and persuasive terms. A fledgling barrister must impersonate a plaintiff who by definition is in the wrong. To such plangent and puerile flights of make-believe these dead letters owe their color and design and their pervasive ambiguity—perhaps their most enduring and endearing aspect. Behind the stagy pathos and bright new learning, the rapid narrative and pithy apothegm, we hear the breaking, eloquent voice of the clever boy who has just begun to shave.

HYPERMNESTRA TO LYNCEUS (XIV)

Hypermnestra was the only one of Danaus' daughters to disobey
his order to kill their bridegroom-cousins on their wedding night.
For this crime of compassion she was imprisoned by her father,
the eponymous ancestor of the ancient Greeks (Danaae). From
her cell in Argos Hypermnestra writes in defiance of her father, in
pity equally for her male cousins slain in their marriage beds and
for her sisters (their murderers), and in tender valediction to her
husband-in-name-only, Lynceus, who got away.

The swift narrative is diverted by a pseudo-Pindaric excursus
on the ancestress of Danaus and his brother Aegyptus, Io, whom
jealous Juno changed into a cow after her seduction by Jove.
Driven to wander the earth, Io at last achieves liberation and
deification in the waters of the Nile.

I write to the sole brother who survives
Of all those immolated by their wives.
Chained, captive in my father's house, I was
Punished because I kept the marriage laws:
For hesitating to dispatch you I'm
Arraigned. What praise could compensate that crime?
Rather blame than such obedience!
I am untroubled by my innocence.
My father's free to torture me, to scorch
Me with my blameless hymeneal torch,
Or murder me with that same sword which I
Refused to use, and now must perish by;
But an apology he'll never get—
A virtuous wife has nothing to regret!

Danaus and my sisters should repent
Their bloody marital experiment:
Bloodthirsty sacrilege, then penitence—
That is the normal sequence of events.

Appalled at the thought of that unholy night
Of blood, my hand shakes so I cannot write;
Afraid to describe a crime I'd not commit,
Though you believed me capable of it,
Still I shall try. Twilight had just descended
And night begun though day had not quite ended,
It was about the hour of crepuscule
When day still lingers in night's vestibule.
Our father-in-law Aegyptus welcomes all
His armed in-laws within Pelasgus' hall.
There lamps of gold are gleaming everywhere;
The scent of sacrilege pollutes the air.
"Hymen!" people call, but He departs;
Connubial Juno too has left these parts.
Fuddled with wine, the bridegrooms, lewd and loud,
Their hair entwined with dewy garlands, crowd
Gaily into their wedding-chamber tombs,
And lay them down to snore in their death rooms.
Oppressed with food and drink they sprawled asleep,
And all about us Argos lay in deep
Repose, when suddenly I seemed to hear
The groans of dying men, so loud and clear
I could not doubt what I had cause to fear.
From mind and body warm blood drained away,
Till frigid on my marriage bed I lay.
Like cornstalks shivering in a chilly breeze
That shakes the leaves upon the poplar trees,

I shivered and shook. You slept through the commotion
For in your wine I'd put a sleeping potion.
Alarmed by father's murderous command,
I rose and shakily took sword in hand;
Three times I raised the sharpened steel, with fell
Intent; three times I lowered it as well;
Against your throat I pressed the blade that my
Father gave; I will not tell a lie:
Timidity and love got in the way,
My innocent right hand would not obey
The wicked order. Tearing out my hair,
Ripping my robe, I whimpered in despair,
"Father's word is law, grim though he is:
It's time to send my bridegroom to join his
Brothers. Yet my gentle maiden's mind
Is not to acts of violence inclined—
Both nature and my youth have made me kind.
Yet why not imitate my sisters' act,
If all their husbands have been slain in fact,
And while he sleeps? But sooner than commit
Bloody murder, I would suffer it.
Their crime? They coveted their uncle's lands—
But ought it not to pass into their hands?
If they deserved to die, then what of us?
What crime prevents my being virtuous?
What's steel to me? or weapons to a maid?
For wool and distaff were these fingers made."
As I spoke, my teardrops flowed amain
And fell upon your drowsy limbs. In vain
You tried to throw your arms about me, and
The murder weapon nearly cut your hand.

Afraid of my father's slaves, about daybreak
I tried to rouse you, whispering, "Awake,
Lynceus, only brother left alive,
Make haste, or else this night you won't survive."
Your lethargy gone, you started up, alarmed
To see me shaking like a leaf—and armed.
"But why . . ."? you asked. "Get going," I explained,
"While it's still dark." You did, but I remained.
Next morning when Danaus came to count
The bodies, yours was missed in the account.
He took it badly that a single son-
In-law survived the massacre of one
And all: "Enough bloodletting's not been done!"
Dragged by my hair from father's knees, I could,
In prison, count the cost of doing good.

Does Juno's ire remain unmollified
Since Io, as a cow, was deified?
Enough, that a gentle girl should stoop to low
And lose her charms for Jupiter, although
She was quite beautiful not long ago.
The new-made heifer on her father's shore
Saw horns where she had not had horns before.
Trying to speak, all she could do was moo,
Alarmed by her looks, and at her diction, too.
Why does your image, Io, so amaze,
Indeed infuriate you as you gaze
At it aghast and try to count your strange
New feet? Why so unhappy at the change?
Dreadful to Juno as Jove's concubine,
Now hungrily on leaves and grass you dine,
And in the stream from which you drink, you stare

In stupefaction at your likeness there,
Afraid of a goring by the horns you wear;
You lie, though Jove paid tribute to your worth
Once, now naked on the naked earth.
Through seas and lands and kindred streams you stray:
No land, no stream, no sea stands in your way.
But what's the purpose in your headlong flight?
Far though you fare you can't escape the sight
Of your own face, which must accompany
You perforce wherever you may flee,
Until the seven mouths of Nile transform
Juno's maddened rival's bovine form.

But why relate these old wives tales, when there
Is plenty in my life to cause despair?
With my father and your own at war,
I'm cast away on this exotic shore.
Your father holds the scepter and the throne:
We carry with us everything we own.
Of all the tribe of brothers, only you
Remain an unimpressive residue.
I pity the slain, and their assassins too.
I've lost as many sisters as you, brothers.
I weep for them as well as for the others.
For saving you I pay the penalty.
What more, if guilty, could they do to me?
When, like all our siblings, I have passed
Away, you'll be the hundredth and the last.
If you are grateful for my piety
And worthy of my generosity,
Bring me aid or death. When I expire
Lay me out upon some secret pyre,

Entomb my ashes with devoted grief
And tears, and let my epitaph be brief:
Hypermnestra died the death deserved
By him whose life in exile she preserved.
See, family values, see how you are served!
I'd write more, but these manacles so chafe
My wrists, I can't; besides, it isn't safe.

CANACE TO MACAREUS (XI)

Nowhere is Ovid's access to mythic material that is now lost to us more apparent than in this little domestic drama. Canace and Macareus, daughter and son of the same stormy father, Aeolus, ruler of the winds, incestuously and furtively produce a son, whose discovery by his grandfather results not only in the infant's exposure and presumed death but also in the compulsory suicide of his mother. The whole story is told in this, her suicide note. Macareus' punishment, implicit in the letter, is no more severe than exile, involuntary or prudential. But exile, which was to be Ovid's own lot, seemed to even the most cosmopolitan ancients a sentence worse than death.

If here or there a word is blotted or
Effaced, it will be by your sister's gore.
Pen in one hand, a drawn sword in the other,
And on her lap a letter to her brother:
Picture Aeolus' daughter thus, as she
Tries to placate her father's cruelty.
I wish that he who ordered my demise
Were here to see it with his very eyes;
Stern as he is, and harsher than his winds,
Without a tear he'd contemplate my wounds.
No doubt from living with his brawling brood
His character reflects their savage mood.
The North, the West, the South he holds in thrall,
And the winged East, the sauciest of all;
He rules the winds but he cannot control

His rage, nor can he regulate his soul.
What if, by birth exalted to the stars,
I number Jove among my avatars?
Nonetheless I grasp this naked blade,
A deadly gift unsuited to a maid.

I wish the hour when first we went to bed
Had been deferred till after I was dead!
Your love for me transcended brotherhood,
To you I meant more than a sister should.
I too caught fire, I thought my heart would melt,
The unknown god I'd heard about I felt;
I lost my healthy colour, I lost weight,
So little and reluctantly I ate.
I hardly slept, each night seemed ages long;
I sighed and groaned though there was nothing wrong.
I did not know the reason for my plight,
Or what love was—but this was love, all right!
My nurse was in her cunning conscious of
My problem first. She said, "You are in love."
I blushed in silence, lowering my eyes,
A gesture that speaks volumes to the wise.
My guilty belly had begun to swell;
My gravid secret made me feel unwell.
What medications did my nurse not bring
To dose me with? She would try anything
That might abort—this much we kept from you—
The thing that deep within my body grew.
Alas! the babe, too vigorous, survived
Whatever tricks its enemy contrived.
Ten times the lovely sister of the sun

Had her resplendent monthly course begun,
When suddenly I felt these strange, acute
New pangs; at giving birth a raw recruit,
I cried aloud. The nurse was shrewd, and so
She hushed me, "You want everyone to know?"
What could I do? My pain compelled a groan
Stifled by fear and shame and that old crone.
I bit my tongue, afraid to moan or speak,
And swallowed the tears that trickled down my cheek.
Death was at hand; bereft of all divine
Aid, an incriminating death was mine.
Distraught with grief you fell on top of me
And clasped me to your bosom ardently.
"My dearest sister, try to live," you cried,
"For more than one would perish if you died.
May hope—for you will be your brother's bride—
Sustain you for our future married life:
The mother of my child will be my wife."
Your words revived me, though I'd died before.
At once the burden of our guilt I bore.

No time to rejoice! Aeolus is at home,
The evidence must be concealed from him.
The midwife hides the baby underneath
The fruit and branches of a votive wreath;
Impressed by her pious mumbo jumbo, king
And populace draw back, unquestioning,
When almost at the door, his wails betray
The babe, who thereby gives himself away.
Aeolus grabs the child, unmasks the ruse,
And makes the palace echo with abuse.

As when the sea is riffled by a breeze
Or when the south wind shakes the aspen trees,
So you might see me tremble and turn white,
The very bed I lay on quaked with fright.
My father's outcry broadcast my disgrace,
He rushed at me and all but slapped my face.
My sole defense was bursting into tears
Of shame and horror, tongue-tied by my fears.

Already he had ordered the poor child
Exposed to wolves and vultures in the wild.
The weak thing wailed, you'd think it understood,
Beseeching him the only way it could.
Imagine my feelings then, dear brother (you,
I'm certain, would have felt the same way too),
Seeing our adversary take away
My heart to feed to savage beasts of prey.
Only when he'd left me did I dare
To wail and beat my breast and tear my hair.
And then Aeolus' henchman, filled with gloom,
Appeared and cruelly pronounced my doom:
"Your father sends this sword," he handed me
The sword, "and says to use it properly."
I take his point, I shall try to be brave
And treasure in my heart the gift he gave.
Is this your wedding present, father? What
A start in life your lucky daughter's got!
Hymen, light no tapers for this bride,
But flee the cursed house of the suicide!
Black furies, scorch me with your wonted fire
And bring your torches to ignite my pyre!

Dear sisters, may you be more fortunate
In whom you wed! Do not forget my fate!

What, a few hours old, could he have done
To vex his grandpapa, my newborn son?
How could he merit death, this innocent?
Mine was the crime, but his the punishment.
Poor babe, his mother's heartbreak, cast away
To be devoured upon the very day
That he was born, the first and last day of
This wretched token of an ill-starred love!
For him I cannot shed a licit tear
Or shave my head in mourning, on his bier
Snatching a last, cold kiss. It is my heart
Rapacious animals will tear apart!
And when I follow my poor baby's shade
With the wound inflicted by this blade,
Hereafter Canace will be believed
Neither a mother long, nor long bereaved.

My brother, once, alas! my fiancé,
Gather the fragments of our son, I pray,
And place them with me in a common tomb:
A little urn should give us ample room.
Remember me as long as you shall live,
Weep on the wounded body of your love,
And faithfully fulfill this last request
When I discharge our father's harsh behest.

HYPSIPYLE TO JASON (VI)

The only dates in mythical time being *before* and *after,* we can place the voyage of the Argo about a generation before the Trojan War, though the cultural gap between those two pseudo-events seems as great as that between fantasy and imagination. The fullest treatment of the Argonautical story, on which Ovid must have drawn, is, however, a Hellenistic pastiche of Homer by Apollonius Rhodius. Outward bound to Colchis, at the eastern end of the Black Sea, Jason and the Argonauts stopped at Lemnos, an ideal feminist society where the women had recently slaughtered all the men, except for the father of Hypsipyle, whose escape that queen effected. The crew of the Argo are nonetheless warmly received and stay at least long enough for their leader, Jason, to father twin children on Hypsipyle before continuing in search of the golden fleece. Too busy, and too successful, to return as promised, Jason, by his overdue absence and rumoured attachment to Medea, bewitching daughter of the king of Colchis (Aeetes) and guardian of the fleece, elicits this hopeless appeal. Hypsipyle's subsequent enslavement and deportation to mainland Greece by raiders results, according to one version, in her association with the foundation of the Nemean games; but she remains one of those marginal people to be found on the verge of great events.

Hypsipyle, (who traces her descent
From Bacchus), she who rules all Lemnos, sent
Word to Jason: what she wrote she meant.
I hear that you have reached your native shore
Again, and with the golden fleece, what's more.
Let me congratulate you, reassured
Of your success—although I wish I'd heard

From you direct—but not a single word!
Well, if you did not stop here on your way
Home, perhaps the winds led you astray?
Whatever the winds, you might have made a sign:
Hypsipyle deserves at least a line.

How did I hear, before your letter came,
You'd yoked the bulls of Mars and made them tame?
From seed you'd sowed a crop of soldiers grew
And slew each other with no help from you;
A watchful dragon kept the fleece secure,
Which nonetheless you managed to secure.
If I could say to disbelievers, "He
Told me so himself," how proud I'd be!
But why should I complain of your neglect?
Remaining yours is all I can expect.

There's some outlandish witch with you, it's said—
A sorceress replaced me in your bed:
But love is blind. What could be sweeter than
Thinking you've wrongfully accused a man.
A traveler called on me the other day
And as he crossed the threshold heard me say,
"How fares my darling Jason?" Then he frowned,
Embarrassed, with his eyes fixed on the ground.
I tore my dress and leapt up with a cry,
"Is he alive? or am I doomed to die?"
"Alive," he gasped; I made him swear it, though
Doubtful of your survival even so.
Reviving, I demanded where—and how?
He told of Mars' bronze bulls put to the plough,
Of serpents' teeth that, scattered on the earth,

Forthwith to full-armed fighting-men gave birth;
An earth-born race, in internecine strife
They died, and in one day lived out their life.
He said that you had slain a dragon, too.
Anxiously again I asked if you
Still lived, and dared not hope that it was true.
But as he told me all the details, he
In his enthusiastic fluency
Revealed how your success has injured me.

What of our vows? the matrimonial
Rites more suited to a funeral?
Ours was no furtive, casual affair:
Juno to bless the marriage bed was there
And Hymen himself with garlands in his hair.
Yet neither, but some grisly Fury bore
Our ill-starred wedding torch imbued with gore.
And what to me were Argo and her crew,
And what my island, anyway, to you?
Here there was no golden fleece to see—
Lemnos is not Aeetes' property.
At first I thought, before fate let me down,
That we could drive the strangers from our town—
Lemnian women can take care of men
All too well!—and keep my virtue. Then
I took one look at you and opened my
Home and heart at once. Two years went by
Till, last autumn, forced to sail away,
Through your tears these words you tried to say:
"Destiny calls! Your husband I'll remain,
Hypsipyle, until we meet again.
Therefore rear with care the infant you

Are carrying. I am its parent too."
Thus far, as I recall, your false face wore
Its mask of tears, but you could speak no more.

You board the sacred Argo last, it flees
With full, distended sails before the breeze;
Beneath the speeding keel blue waves run free.
You gaze toward the land; I, out to sea.
The tower where I hid myself and cried
Overlooks the waves on every side.
I peer through tears, and yet my eyes, infused
With longing, see much further than they used.
And what of my pure prayers, that fearful vow
Which, now you're safe, I'm bound by anyhow?
Must I fulfill them for Medea's sake?
With love and rage my heart is like to break.
Am I to offer up a holocaust
For you and everything that I have lost?

In fact I never felt secure, afraid
Lest Aeson wed you to some Argive maid;
I feared the Greeks, but in a sneak attack
Some foreign slut has stabbed me in the back.
Neither her beauty nor enchanting parts
Beguile you, but her necromantic arts.
She knows all charms, and with her magic blade
Reaps noxious herbs that flourish in the shade.
She strives to conjure down the struggling moon
Off course, and to eclipse the sun at noon.
She checks the waters of meandering streams
And can displace whole woods and rocks, it seems.
With snaky locks she strays amid gravestones,

From smoldering pyres collecting human bones.
To cast a spell she shapes a mannequin
From wax, which she transfixes with a pin—
And God knows what! But love is rudely wooed
With charms, instead of charm and pulchritude.
Could you embrace this woman as your bride,
Or know a quiet moment at her side?
As if you were a bullock, she can make
You bear the yoke; she charms you like a snake.
What's more, Medea's version of your story
Gives her the hero's share of all the glory.
Your enemies ascribe your triumphs to
Her witchcraft—many folk believe them, too.
"Aeetes' daughter, not old Aeson's son
Took Phrixus' fleece, when all is said and done."
Your parents won't approve—ask their advice—
A bride you bring them from the realms of ice.
Let her find a husband nearer home,
Where on the steppes barbaric nomads roam.

O Jason, fickle as the air in spring,
Doesn't your promised word mean anything?
You were my husband when you went away,
But now? I am your wife still, anyway.
Does noble birth impress you? Look at mine,
Thoas' daughter born of Minos' line;
My granddam, Bacchus' bride, by Bacchus crowned,
Outshines the lesser constellations round.
Lemnos is mine to give you, all my lands—
I do not come to you with empty hands.
And now I've given birth, you, Jason, should
Congratulate us both. How sweet and good,

For your sake, seemed the pangs of motherhood!
Moreover, I was doubly lucky, for
Twins were the twofold pledge of love I bore.
You ask whom they are like? You'd recognize
Yourself in them—except they don't tell lies.
About to send them both to plead my cause,
The thought of their stepmother gave me pause.
I fear Medea: worse than a stepmother,
She's capable of some abuse or other.
Would she, who cut her brother up to strew
His bits about, be kind to my babes, too?
This woman you, deranged by sorcery,
Prefer, it's said, to your Hypsipyle!
This wanton virgin took you to her bed
Illicitly—you are already wed!
She tricked her father; I refused to kill
Mine; though she levanted, I'm here still.
What good is virtue? Wicked women win
And purchase husbands dowered with their sin.
The Lemnian womens' actions I condemn,
Though not astonished at their stratagem:
Weak as they were, their suffering armed them.

Confess, if you and every Argonaut
Were forced into this harbour, as you ought
To be, and saw me and the children too,
Wouldn't you wish the earth would swallow you?
How could you face your babes and me, you wretch?
What price but death should breach of promise fetch?
Nevertheless, though worthless, you would find
Forgiveness here, but just because I'm kind.
But as for her! that sorceress! that whore

Who stole your heart from me by magic! your
Eyes and mine will batten on her gore!
I'll out-Medea her! O God, if there
Be any judge on high to hear my prayer,
Make this interloper suffer in
The same way I do, and just to begin
With, give her a taste of her own medicine!
As I, a wife and mother, have been left,
May she of spouse and children be bereft,
And soon, an outcast justly stripped of her
Ill-got gains, a homeless wanderer.
So cruel to her brother, may she be
Equally harsh to her young family,
Then hopeless, hapless, all bloodstained with their
Slaughter, having quite in her despair
Exhausted sea and land, take to the air.
This is my prayer, dishonestly unwed:
Curse man and wife in their devoted bed!

MEDEA TO JASON (XII)

There is nothing marginal about Medea, whose name signifies intelligence and cunning. Enchanting daughter of Aeetes, king of Colchis, she was also niece of Circe, whose magic Odysseus narrowly escapes, and, like Ariadne and Phaedra, grandaughter of the sun. As well versed in the black arts, including pharmacology, as she is well connected, Medea aids Jason in stealing the golden fleece by means of a series of tests, detailed here, which highlight the fairy-tale quality of this saga. She then accompanies him to Greece, where she tricks the daughters of King Pelias, who had set the whole quest afoot, into attempting to rejuvenate him by cutting him up and boiling him in a magic cauldron. Medea, however, withholds the secret ingredient, with predictable fatal results. When Jason imprudently deserts her for Creusa, Medea takes the terrible revenge threatened at the end of this letter, incinerating her rival, immolating her children by Jason, and flying off to Athens in a dragon-chariot. Ovid wrote a tragedy—which unlike its heroine has not survived—on this subject, and he refers to it in several other letters. It is no wonder that this is the most dramatic of his monologues.

> While queen of Colchis, I believe, I made
> Available to you my magic aid.
> That was the period at which the dread
> Sisters should have cut my mortal thread
> Short, for then I could have died content:
> Existence since seems one long punishment.
>
> Cursed be the day the gilded youth of Greece
> Aboard the Argo sought the golden fleece!

When we in Colchis saw this foreign ship
Crowded with heroes in our Phasis dip
Oar! just why your beauty charmed me so,
Fair hair and fair, false tongue, I do not know.
O why, when that strange ship had come to land
And had discharged its brash, adventurous band,
Didn't heartless Jason meet his death
Unarmed against the bronze bulls' fiery breath?
Or plant a fatal foe with every seed
And therefore reap what he had sown indeed?
What bad faith would have perished, rogue, with you!
How many woes would have been spared me too!

There is a certain pleasure—is there not?—
In bringing up old benefits forgot?
And I intend to savour what may be
The only pleasure you can give to me.
Untried, obedient to some command,
You trespassed in my happy fatherland.
Medea in that country occupied
The same position as your newest bride
In this; in father's wealth I too took pride:
Hers rules the shores of Corinth; my papa
Reigns from the Hellespont to Scythia.
Aeetes welcomed you; your shipmates made
Themselves at home upon our rich brocade.
I saw you; even though you were unknown
To me, my peace of mind was overthrown.
I looked and was lost, I burned with strange, divine
Fire, like a pine torch blazing in a shrine.
Irresistible as destiny

And handsome, with a look you ravished me.
I think you guessed, you wretch! for there's no way
Of hiding love; it gives itself away.

Then you were told our laws: that you somehow
Must break two untamed oxen to the plough.
(The bulls belonged to Mars, their igneous
Breath as well as horns were dangerous.
Their feet were solid brass, each brazen snout
Was blackened by the flames that they breathed out.)
You were commanded furthermore to sow
The fields with seeds from which a host would grow
To attack you, earthborn men at arms,
A disconcerting crop for one who farms!
Your final task: by any means you can
To dupe the fleece's sleepless guardian.
So said the king. You Argonauts in woe
From your purple couches rose to go.
How far away Creusa seemed to you
Then, her father and her dowry too!
Sadly you left. A tear bedimmed my eye,
Seeing you depart; I sighed, "Goodbye!"

Smitten, I sought my bed, then—not to sleep
But all night long to lie awake and weep.
The bulls—the watchful snake—the dreadful crop
Plagued my imagination without stop,
Whence fear, then love—but love was fed by fear.
Next morning, entering my room, my dear
Sister perceived my pitiable case
From my disheveled hair and tear-stained face.

She begged me anyway I could to save
The Argonauts . . . the aid she asked I gave.

Pines and oaks obscure a certain glade
So sunbeams rarely penetrate its shade:
There is—or was—a temple in that wood
Where chaste Diana's golden statue stood:
Have you forgotten that as well as me?
For there you first committed perjury!
"Yours to decree what destiny demands:
Henceforth my life and death are in your hands.
Great as appears your power to hurt at will,
My preservation would be greater still.
Since you can solve my problems I implore
You, by your family's solar ancestor,
And by the rites of great Diana, and
Whatever gods are honored in this land,
O maiden, pity me and mine, and make
Me yours eternally, for pity's sake.
But if you will not deign to wed a Greek—
Dare I such heavenly condescension seek?—
May my spirit melt into thin air
Before another bride than you shall share
My bed! Witness Juno who presides
Over the vows of bridegrooms and of brides,
Also the goddess in whose marble fane
We're standing, that I do not swear in vain!"
The speech of which these words are but a part,
Your handclasp, touched a simple maiden's heart.
I even saw you weep—is there a way
Of feigning tears? The things you had to say
Thus quickly stole my maidenhead away.

You brought the brazen bulls beneath the yoke
Unscathed, and then the hard-packed ploughland broke,
Using that plough of which my father spoke.
With deadly dragons' teeth you sowed the earth,
And soldiers sprang up, fully armed from birth,
And even I, who'd lent my magic aid,
Paled to see so suddenly arrayed
That miraculously earth-born band
In fratricidal combat hand to hand.
Behold the sleepless, giant loathly worm
Hiss and on his scaly belly squirm!
Where was the dowry of your royal bride,
The isthmus with the sea on either side,
When I, outlandish as I seem to you
Nowadays, and poor, and baleful too,
Cast on those blazing eyes a drowsy spell
And helped you safely snatch the fleece as well?

My father I betrayed, his realm forsook:
Exile as my just deserts I took.
I left my sister and my mother, gave
Myself, a virgin, to an errant knave.
I sacrificed my brother to our flight
Ruthlessly, but more I cannot write,
The deed I dared to do defies my pen:
I too should have been torn in pieces then!
Nor did I fear the sea—why, after all,
Should I, a woman and a criminal?

Where's the heavenly retribution we
So thoroughly deserved to meet at sea—
You for deceit, I for credulity?

Why didn't the Symplegades collide
To mash our bones together side by side?
Why did rapacious Scylla, who must loathe
All ingrates, not make mincemeat of us both?
Or Charybdis' whirlpool drag us down
Under the Sicilian sea to drown?

In triumph, safe returned against all odds,
You laid the golden fleece before your gods.
Why mention Pelias' pious daughters, who
Were hoodwinked by my demonstration to
Chop their father up to make a stew?
To you I'll praise myself, since others blame
The crimes that I committed in your name.
But then you dared—words fail me, yes, I grieve
To say—you dared to order me to leave!
I left, and took our children with me, and
That love that drives me over sea and land.

Too soon I seemed to hear the marriage choir
As torches blazed with hymeneal fire
And flutes poured forth your wedding melody,
Alas! more doleful than a dirge to me!
I had not known there was such wickedness,
But I turned cold with horror nonetheless,
And still the crowd's enthusiastic cheers,
Drawing ever nearer, hurt my ears.
Covertly my slaves were all in tears
On every side, for nobody could choose
To be the messenger of such bad news.
Whatever it was, I did not want to know;

My heart was sore with knowing even so.
My younger son, agog to see the show,
Called me to the window, "Mummy, see
Daddy's leading the parade—there he
Goes in all his golden finery!"
At that I beat my breast and tore my dress
And even scratched my face in my distress.
My fury prompted me to rush outside
And snatch the wedding garland off your bride;
Beside myself, I almost could have thrown
My arms about you, claimed you as my own.

Father, rejoice! Forsaken and betrayed,
Thus I propitiate my brother's shade!
Having lost my home and native land,
I find myself at last abandoned and
Humiliated by my husband—he
Who hitherto was all in all to me.
Wild bulls and serpents I could subjugate,
One creature I could not subdue: my mate.
Although my spells protected him from fire,
I can't escape the ardours of desire;
My magic arts are gone, enchantment fails,
Not even mighty Hecate avails.
Daylight I loathe, I lie awake all night,
Uncomforted by sleep however slight,
And I, who could a dragon hypnotize,
Cannot induce myself to close my eyes
With drugs that proved so potent otherwise.
The limbs I saved another's limbs entwine:
The prize is hers, the effort all was mine.

Perhaps when boasting to your foolish wife
You will find something in my way of life
Or appearance possibly to blame?
Well, let her laugh and vilify my name,
Let her exult in purple! Soon she will
Weep, and burn with fiercer passions still.
As long as there is poison, steel, or fire,
Medea's enemies shall feel her ire!
Listen, if prayer can touch a breast of steel,
To words that fall far short of all I feel.
Today I come as supplicant to you,
And kneel at your feet, just as you used to do
At mine in supplication—often, too!
Think of our sons, though you think ill of me;
Protect them from Creusa's savagery.
They trouble me—how like you they appear!
Each time I look at them, I shed a tear.
By the gods and my forebear, the sun,
By our babes and everything I've done
For you, give back your love, which I was mad
Enough to buy with everything I had!
Be true to your word, remembering your vow,
And if I ever helped you, help me now.
I do not seek your aid with man or bull
Or to make a snake insensible,
It's you I seek, I have deserved your love
Which you yourself made me a present of.

You ask, where is my dowry? Need you ask?
Did I not assist you in your task?
My dowry is the golden fleece, which I
Know, if I asked it back, you would deny.

My dowry is your safety and the health
Of all your crew. Has Creon's girl such wealth?
Your life, your marriage, your prosperity—
And your ingratitude!—you owe to me,
And soon enough . . . but why should I say more?
My anger has enormities in store,
Which I'll pursue. Perhaps I shall repent
In time the manner of your punishment,
Yet what is worthier repentance than
Having cared for such a callous man?
Let that deity see to the rest
Who causes such a turmoil in my breast,
As I elaborate I don't know what
Awful scheme too terrible for thought!

DEIANIRA TO HERCULES (IX)

The most popular of ancient heroes, Hercules embarked with the Argo but jumped ship en route, distraught over the disappearance of his catamite, Hylas. After adventures and labors too numerous to mention—many undertaken at the instance of one Eurystheus, agent of Hera, the cruel stepmother whose true relationship is hinted at by Hercules' Greek name, Heracles (glory of Hera)—he marries Deinira, an apparently innocuous water nymph. The centaur Nessus attempts to ravish her, and Hercules kills him: but, dying, Nessus persuades Deianira to take some of his blood as an aphrodisiac or love philter. When eventually Hercules abandons her for a younger girl, Iole, Deianira dips a garment in the centaur's blood, and Hercules puts it on—with fatal results.

Of the adventures and misadventures of Hercules alluded to here, too briefly to merit elucidation, Hercules' transvestite servitude to Queen Omphale of Lydia seems to have excited Ovid's interest, as it did Deianira's jealousy, for he also treats it in the second book of his *Fasti*.

> I'm glad to hear Ochalia's annexed,
> But your perverse behavior has me vexed.
> A shocking rumor is in circulation—
> Quite inconsistent with your reputation—
> That you, whom Juno's labors never broke,
> Have now submitted to Iole's yoke.
> Eurystheus of course will hope it's true,
> And Juno, your unkind stepmother, who
> Delights in all aspersions cast on you,
> But he who in no single night begot

Your singular preeminence, will not.
Venus, not Juno, is your enemy:
Exalted by the one's severity,
You grovel before the other's levity.

Behold the world your strength has pacified
As far as Ocean's all-embracing tide.
Securing land and sea, your deeds have won
You glory everywhere beneath the sun:
You shouldered heaven, soon to be your home,
When you like Atlas bore the starry dome.
If to these deeds you add a deed of shame,
You will bring foul disgrace upon your name.
Your father's son, did you, in swaddling bands,
Not strangle two huge snakes in your bare hands?
Alas! You've finished worse than you began:
The child was very different from the man!
You, whom a thousand monsters could not beat,
Or Juno, faced with love admit defeat.
Yet wedding you I "married well," for my
Father-in-law's the Thunderer on high.
As with an ill-matched team, a humble spouse
Is chafed by marriage to a royal house,
No honor but an onerous counterfeit
Harmful to those who have to bear with it;
An alliance of equals always seems more fit.
My husband's like a guest in his own home;
In search of monsters he prefers to roam.
I say my lonely prayers, afraid lest he
Fall victim to some frightful enemy;
With roaring lions, boars, and horrible
Snakes and three-headed dogs my nights are full.

Nightmares, omens, presages affright
Me, all the occult mysteries of night;
To rumor's vagaries I lend an ear
As fear succeeds to hope, and hope to fear.
Your mother's elsewhere, sorry to have won
The favor of a god; Amphitryon,
Your father, isn't here, nor is our son.
I sense behind Eurystheus the weight
Of Juno arbitrarily irate.

As if that's not enough, you foist on me
The fruits of your errant promiscuity,
An epidemic of maternity.
I need not tell how Auge was beguiled
And Astydamia was got with child,
Nor charge you with those fifty sisters, of
Whom not one was cheated of your love.
One outrage only shall I dwell upon,
Your recent liaison with that Amazon.
Meander as it twists upon its track,
Its weary waters always turning back,
Saw, astonished, necklaces bedeck
Hercules' sturdy, sky-supporting neck.
Shamelessly you braceleted your arms,
Embellishing with gems your brawny charms—
To think that those same arms had strength to slay
Nemea's scourge, whose hide you wear today!
You even wound a turban round your hair—
A poplar garland would look better there!
Nor, like a harlot, did you think it wrong
To dress up in a Lydian sarong—

Did you remember Diomedes then
That brute who fed his mares the flesh of men?
Busiris would be mortified to brag
How he was worsted by a man in drag;
Antaeus would pull your beads off rather than
Be beaten by so sissified a man.
They say that you sat spinning, too, afraid
Of being scolded, trembling like a maid.
Your mighty hand, Alcides, did not shirk,
After a thousand labors, woman's work,
Hoping, as your clumsy fingers teased
The thread, the handsome housewife would be pleased.
How often your hands, not knowing their own strength,
Must have snapped the fine-spun linen's length!
It's said, poor wretch, that at your lady's feet you
Cowered terrified that she would beat you,
And told her extraordinary feats
Of prowess that no gentleman repeats,
Like how in infancy you strangled two
Giant serpents sent to strangle you,
And how you slew the Erymanthine boar
Whose monstrous weight laid waste the forest floor.
Neither the man-eating equine race
Whose heads you offered to the gods of Thrace,
Nor that triple monster Geryon
Did you forget, uniquely three-in-one.
You told of Cerberus, that hellish hound,
Each of his three heads with vipers crowned;
And Hydra, who, beheaded, grew a new
Head, the more you cut the more they grew;

And, crushed between your arm and side, the great
Antaeus, a hung-up, helpless heavyweight;
And of those horse-men whom, egregriously
Proud of their hooves and their biformity,
You banished from the heights of Thessaly:
You told all this, so gorgeously bedecked:
Did not your costume ruin the effect?

Your martial gear the fair virago wore
In turn, like famous trophies won in war.
Go on, boast of your brave exploits to her—
She's more of a hero than you ever were!
Her triumph over you is just the same
As overcoming what you overcame.
Here is the glory of your deeds—prepare
To yield all to your ladyfriend and heir.
O shame! that a hairy lion's rugged pelt
Should swathe a female form so soft and svelte!
But there you are mistaken, badly too:
That is no lion's skin, but yours! You slew
The beast, but she has stripped the hide from you!
Almost unequal to the household arts,
This woman held your weighty poisoned darts;
She grasped your monstrous club's death-dealing mass
And posed in your armor in her looking-glass.

To disregard such hearsay I was free;
This new affront is all too plan to see:
Your foreign concubine offends my eyes,
I cannot hide my horror and surprise.
Your "captive" you parade in public so

I have to see her, willingly or no;
Not like other prisoners, her face
Veiled by her hair proclaiming her disgrace—
No, she struts, a vision to behold,
Ablaze, like you in Phrygia, with gold,
Bold-faced, head high, as if you had in fact
Been conquered and her city stood intact.
And then, once Deianira's driven out,
She'll change from concubine to wife, no doubt!
A scandalous marriage will unite these twain,
Iole and Hercules, for he's insane.
The awful premonition strikes me dumb;
My hands lie in my lap inert and numb.
You loved me too, though not exclusively;
Our love could boast respectability,
And twice, you must admit, you fought for me.
Weeping Acheloüs hides his head,
Now hornless, in his muddy riverbed.
The centaur Nessus poisoned with his blood
In his death throes swift Evenus' flood—

■

What? Even as I wrote, the story came
That you had perished in a robe of flame
I'd dipped in Nessus' blood. Am I to blame?
Love drove me to this frenzy. Why should I,
Guilty of murder, hesitate to die?

Seeing my husband flayed and burnt alive,
Shall I who am responsible survive?
What have I got to show I was your wife?

To seal our marriage I shall take my life,
And prove I'm Meleager's sister. Why
Should Deianira hesitate to die?

Our race is doomed: my uncle seized the throne;
Dethroned, my aged father starves alone;
One brother exiled in an unknown land,
The other's life hung on a smoldering brand;
Our mother stabbed herself to death, so why
Does Deianira hesitate to die?

Only believe me for our past love's sake,
I didn't mean to, it was a mistake,
For Nessus told me with his dying breath
His blood had power to conjure love, not death,
And so I smeared it on your garment. Why,
Deianira, hesitate to die?

Father, farewell, and sister Gorge, and
My banished brother! Farewell, fatherland!
Husband, farewell! I only wish you may
Fare well! And for our little son I pray,
Gazing my last upon the light of day.

ARIADNE TO THESEUS (X)

The death of his son Androgeus at Athenian hands was the pretext
of the annual tribute exacted by King Minos of Crete. This were-
gild consisted of seven youths and seven maidens to be devoured
by the minotaur, monstrous offspring of Minos' queen, Pasiphae,
and a bull. Son of Aegeus, king of Athens—or of Poseidon, for like
many heroes he boasted both human and divine parentage—
Theseus joined what was to prove the last such shipment, thanks
to him. With the aid of Ariadne, daughter of Minos and Pasiphae,
he sought out and slew the hybrid in his labyrinthine lair, from
which he escaped by retracing the thread she gave him. His grati-
tude proved short-lived, however, and on the way back to Athens
Theseus abandoned Ariadne on an inhospitable island, where
eventually she found solace with the god of wine.

I'm writing to you from that island whence
You set sail without me. In a sense,
I was betrayed by sleep and you: it seems
You stalked me in the labyrinth of dreams.
A savage beast compared to you is kind.
Than you, what worse protector could I find?

It was that time when dew upon the grass
First sparkles with the brilliance of glass
And birds beneath the leaves begin to peep.
Lying half-awake and half-asleep,
I stretched my arms out drowsily to where
Thesus lay—but there was no one there!
Snatching back my hand, I tried again,

Ransacked the bedding high and low—in vain!
Terror banished sleep; I leapt in dread
Precipitately from my empty bed.
Ah, then I beat my breast in my despair
And wildly tore my sleep-disheveled hair.
The moon was up; I gazed toward the shore,
But I could see the beach and nothing more.
To and fro I ran distracted, and
My girlish footsteps stumbled in the sand,
And all the while I called your name, and all
The cliffs around the bay returned my call:
"Theseus!" the scenery when I
Cried out would sympathetically reply.

A cliff there was nearby, with on its top
A shrub or two, eroded, a sheer drop:
I climbed it, given strength by my emotion,
And from that vantage point surveyed the ocean,
And there, a victim of the elements,
I saw the south wind wafting you from hence—
At least I thought I saw it. In a trice
I fell down half-alive and cold as ice.
Grief did not let me languish long; I came
To, aghast, and loudly called your name:
"Theseus, what's your hurry? Turn your fleet
Around, the manifest is not complete."
The gaps between my gasps I filled with groans,
And mangled phrases mingled with my moans.
Hoping that if you couldn't hear me you
Could see me still, I waved and signaled too,
And tied white rags to poles, just to remind
You of the girl you went and left behind.

You'd disappeared already. Then I cried,
Whom sorrow hitherto had kept dry-eyed.
For what but tears could my poor eyes avail
Once they lost sight of your retreating sail?
Alternately I raved and ran around
Like a Maenad with my hair unbound,
Or gazing seaward, on a rock alone
I sat, as cold and motionless as stone.
Often I sought the bed we used to share,
Never again to welcome such a pair,
And tried to trace your imprint on the sheet
That in your place still held your body's heat.
Face-down, I soaked the pillow with a tear:
"Where are they now who lay together here?
Coupled, we came; uncoupled, we depart.
Unfaithful bed, where is my better part?"

What shall I do? How bear my solitude?
This island is unpopulated, rude,
Also apparently devoid of food,
On every side surrounded by the sea,
And not a ship in the vicinity.
Even with a crew, a vessel, and
Fair winds—where could I sail? You understand
I am not welcome in my fatherland!
Though over tranquil seas my barque may roam
Favored by gentle gales, I have no home.
Never again, alas, shall I behold
Crete's hundred cities, known to Jove of old.
My father and the kingdom that he swayed
With his just rule, I wickedly betrayed
By giving you, to guide you from the maze,

A thread to lead you through its winding ways.
You swore, "By all the perils we've been through,
As long as we both live I shall be true."
Well, I'm alive; assuming you are too,
Where is your troth? Your promise was a cheat!
I am entombed by Theseus' deceit.
You should have killed me and my brother both:
Our deaths would have absolved you of your oath.

Not only do I contemplate my own
Grim fate, but any woman's left alone.
A thousand ways of dying leap to mind;
Waiting for death is worse than death, I find.
Already, circling me I scent a pack
Of wolves that raven, ready to attack;
There may, who knows, be lions near at hand,
Perhaps man-eating tigers prowl this land?
They say huge seals are cast up by the tide.
If there are men, there may be homicide.
Anything except captivity,
Enchainment, and domestic drudgery!
I, Minos' daughter, scion of the sun,
And, more important far, your promised one!
Gazing over sea and shore, I sense
Both sea's and land's immense malevolence,
I dread the gods emblazoned in the sky.
Abandoned, food for beasts of prey am I.
Had I neighbors, I'd distrust them then,
Taught by experience to fear strange men.

O that Androgeos had never died
And Cecrops' city had not satisfied

The claims of justice with a nation's pride!
High-handed Theseus, if only your
Stout cudgel hadn't slain the minotaur,
And I had never shown you how to find
The exit, giving you a string to wind
Up! Of course the monster in defeat
Was stretched out lifeless on the soil of Crete:
Your heart of iron saved you from the bull,
Your naked breast was quite invincible,
As adamant or flint impervious
Or something even harder, Theseus!

O cruel sleep, why did you hold me tight
And not consign me to eternal night?
O cruel winds, too favorable too,
To make me weep how briskly then you blew!
O meaningless pledge, delivered on demand!
My brother and I, despatched by the same hand!
By sleep and winds and words was I undone:
The odds were in your favour, three to one.
Thus when I die I cannot hope to see
My mother's tears, and none shall bury me;
My ghost shall wander through the atmosphere
With no kind hand to lay me on my bier.
Will seabirds my unburied bones consume?
My kindnesses deserve a better tomb!
When you are welcomed in your fatherland
And raised above the listening people stand
Telling of the minotaur's demise,
The doubtful turnings of the stony maze,
Tell how I was abandoned here: my name
Should add a little luster to your fame.

No, Aethra to Aegeus never bore
You, but the harsh sea and rocky shore.

If only you had seen me from your deck,
You couldn't be unmoved by such a wreck.
Try to imagine my despair and grief,
Clinging to this inundated reef,
My hair unkempt as if in mourning, my
Garments soaked with tears that never dry.
I shiver like a wind-swept wheatfield, and
Scrawl this letter in a shaky hand.
I shall not plead my just deserts, for they
Have proven my undoing anyway;
But, though unworthy of acknowledgment,
Did my good deeds deserve such punishment?
And even if I didn't help you, why
On that account abandon me to die?
Tired of beating my poor breast in vain,
I stretch my hands to you across the main.
See how in grief I've torn out half my hair!
As you provoked my tears, now hear my prayer;
Theseus, turn back! Reverse your course!
If I am dead, collect my bones, of course.

PHAEDRA TO HIPPOLYTUS (IV)

Ariadne's sister Phaedra forms a more lasting but hardly happier marriage with the ubiquitous Theseus, to whom she bears sons, one of whom, Demophoön, is the recipient of another letter from another unhappy woman, Phyllis (II). Phaedra falls in love with her stepson Hippolytus, Theseus' son by the amazon Hippolyta; he—for various, surely superfluous, reasons—repels the advances of his stepmother. The results as well as the motives of his impasse vary as widely as their treatment by poets from Euripides to Racine, to mention only the most distinguished to whom the quasi-incestuous situation has seemed irresistible.

This Cretan bride salutes the manly boy
Who, only, has the power to bring her joy.
Read it all—what harm can letters do?
There even may be something here for you.
By writing, secrets spread to foreign lands,
And enemies read one another's hands.
Three times I tried to speak to you and found
My useless tongue too dumb to make a sound.
Love should be seemly, when it can and may:
Love bids me write what I'm ashamed to say.
Love's orders would be risky to ignore,
Whom even the almighty gods adore.
At first I hesitated. Love said, "Write!
For all his armor he'll give up the fight."
May Love stand by me! Having pierced me through
And through, I pray he'll plant his darts in you.
I shall not flout my marriage vows in thoughtless

Haste: my honor hitherto was spotless,
But love delayed is far more serious.
I burn with passions blind and furious.
As bullocks to the yoke hate to submit
And wild young horses bridle at the bit,
A heart unbroken chafes at its first love
Which imposition I'm impatient of.
Misconduct learned since youth becomes a knack
Whereof late-blooming lovers feel the lack.
You'll take the bloom off my unsullied name,
Yet in a sense we both shall be to blame.
Of course it's nice to gather up a few
Windfalls, and pick roses fresh with dew.
Well, if my purity, which I maintained
Above reproach, must after all be stained,
I'm glad I'm not besotted with some cad.
Adultery itself is not so bad.
My sweetheart I prefer to any other,
Including Juno's mighty spouse and brother.

I've lately taken up some new pursuits
You won't believe—pursuing savage brutes.
Diana with her bow I reverence,
Eager to share your every preference.
I love to scour the woods for game and ride
After the hounds across the mountainside,
To hurl a sturdy spear with all my strength,
Or stretch out on the greensward at full length,
Or turn a racing chariot and rein
Galloping horses on the dusty plain.
At times I am transported, like bacchants
Or Cybele's enthusiasts who dance

Under Ida, mystic celebrants,
Or those who know what panic is, who fled
From nymphs and fauns in superstitious dread.
Informed of everything when I recover,
I burn in silence like a knowing lover.
Perhaps I'm doomed by my heredity,
This tribute Love takes from my family.
By sleeping with Europa Jove began
(Disguised as a bull) the saga of our clan.
My mother, Pasiphae, seduced a bull,
And she gave birth to something horrible.
Theseus escaped, but never paid
My sister Ariadne for her aid.
Now I, lest you should doubt that Minos was
My father, serve the same genetic laws.
It must be fate! Two sisters drawn to one
Family: Ariadne was undone
By your father, I fell for his son.
The son of Theseus and Theseus
Have scored a double triumph over us.

That time we visited Eleusis—how
I wish I'd never left my homeland now!
For then it was I found you even more
Attractive than I thought you were before,
And, daggerlike, love pierced me to the core.
Dressed all in white, you wore a floral wreath,
A bashful blush suffused your skin beneath
Its golden glow. The harshness some see in
Your face impresses me as masculine.
I don't like youths effeminately dressed;
A simple toilet suits male beauty best.

Roughness becomes you, not each hair in place,
But manly grime upon your handsome face.
When you break in a stubborn stallion, I
Admit your flexing muscles catch my eye,
And when your fist is brandishing a lance
Your potent arm attracts and holds my glance;
If you take up the weapons of the chase—
Well, you regale my sight in any case.
But leave your harshness in the wilderness:
Must I expire of your hard-heartedness?
What good is exercise, though it delights
Diana, that cheats Venus of her rights?
Nothing without rest and change can stand;
Repose restores us on the other hand.
Even Diana's bow, however taut—
Like yours—must slacken sometime, must it not?
Cephalus was famed the forest through
Because of all the animals he slew,
Yet he did not resist Aurora's whim
When, leaving her old man, she came to him.
Some plot of grass, with oak trees overhead,
Was often Venus' and Adonis' bed.
Meleager with the present of
A boar's head purchased Atalanta's love.
Now let us imitate each happy pair.
Your woods are wild if Venus isn't there.
I'll seek you out, unfazed by caverns or
Fear of the tusked and terrifying boar.

A narrow isthmus two broad seas divides
And hears their breakers roaring on both sides;
There will I live with you, on Troezen's strand,

In Pittheus' kingdom, which is kinder and
More pleasing to me than my fatherland.
Neptune's grandson is away, and will
Be for a while, with Pirithoös still,
His friend, whom Theseus apparently
Continues to prefer to you and me.
That's not the only wrong he's done to us:
The things that we endure are hideous.
He broke my brother's bones in bits to strew
The labyrinth, and left my sister to
The mercy of wild beasts. The woman who
Bore you, most valiant of amazons,
Whose bravery was equal to her son's—
What was her fate? Your father slew his wife;
Not even having you could save her life.
She was not wed according to our rites,
All to deprive a bastard of his rights;
It wasn't my idea to educate
My sons, your brothers, as legitimate:
Rather than harm the dearest boy on earth
I wish that I had died in giving birth!
Continue to respect the marriage bed
Which Theseus in fact renounced and fled,
If you insist; but why should incest shock
You? Don't believe that pious poppycock:
Nowadays such scruples seem as old-
Fashioned as the fabled age of gold.
Jove, who proclaimed all pleasure sanctified,
To prove it took his sister for his bride.
Family ties are strengthened, and a lot
More intimate, when Venus ties the knot.

As for discretion, our relationship
Will cover our relations, should we slip:
If someone saw us kissing one another
They'd praise me as a dutiful stepmother.
No need for you to sneak into the house
At midnight, to deceive my watchful spouse,
For this will be our home as heretofore,
You'll kiss me openly just as before.
You're safe with me; you would be praised instead
Of blamed, were you discovered in my bed.
But hurry, so the hasty consummation
Of our desires may spare you my frustration.

I'm not too grand to grovel to you. How
Abject! What price my proud professions now?
I thought I should be able to resist
Temptation—does such strength of mind exist?
Vanquished but royal, I embrace your knees:
A lover overlooks the decencies,
And shame forsakes its standards on the field.
Forgive my frankness, heart of stone, and yield!
What though my father Minos rules the sea?
What use his father's thunderbolts to me?
What use that ancestor whose brilliant rays
And chariot of crimson warm our days?
High birth is trumped by love. Though pitiless
To me, think of my ancestors' distress.
My heritage, Jove's royal island, Crete,
I lay it all at my dear stepson's feet.
Listen, my mother could corrupt a bull:
Are you more fiercely incorruptible?
Pity, for Venus' sake! Do not disdain

Me, and I pray you'll never love in vain.
Nimble Diana hasten to your aid
When you are hunting in some distant glade,
And, steadying your arm, improve your aim.
And may the woods afford you heaps of game.
May satyrs and Pans, those mountain gods, appear
To guide you, boars fall victim to your spear.
Likewise may nymphs, though you, it's said, have cursed
Their sex, bring water to assuage your thirst.
These prayers I seal with tears. When all is said
And done, and you from end to end have read
This letter, think what tears its author shed.

OENONE TO PARIS (V)

This and the following seven letters provide feminine footnotes to the *Iliad* and the *Odyssey*, which furnished much material to Greek and Latin poets, evidence of the greater durability and appeal of myth transformed into literature. The nymph Oenone, first love of Paris, son of King Priam of Troy and erstwhile foundling and shepherd, reproaches him with deserting her as a consequence of a beauty competition among three goddesses, Juno, Minerva (Pallas), and Venus. As a reward for awarding the golden apple to Venus, Paris was encouraged to seek the love of the most beautiful woman in the world (according to her who should know): Helen, already married to Menelaus, king of Sparta. He does so—with notorious, incalculable consequences. The lives of nymphs, though naturally long, were neither endless nor usually eventful. Summoned, toward the end of the Trojan War, to treat the fatally wounded instigator of it all with the medical skills inculcated in her by Appollo, Oenone will refuse until too late, and in remorse will immolate herself on Paris' funeral pyre.

> The nymph whom Paris swears he never knew
> From lofty Ida sends these scribbled few
> Words to him to whom she still is true.
> Will your new bride let you read this? Do so—
> It's not in Mycenean Greek, you know.
> A water nymph, Oenone, I lament
> The wrong you did me, dear—with your consent?
> What god has cursed me? What injustice will
> Prevent my staying your beloved still?
> Merited punishment is bearable;
> What one has not deserved is terrible.

You weren't so grand when I, the daughter of
A mighty river, granted you my love.
Though Priam's son, you were (to tell the truth)
A slave. A nymph, I wed that servile youth.
Amongst your flocks we often rolled at ease
On beds of leafy grass beneath the trees,
And sometimes while we lay on straw and hay
A lowly cabin kept the frost away.
Who pointed out the woods that suit the chase
Best, and the bear cubs' rocky hiding place?
At times I helped you spread your snares around,
Or hunted with swift hounds on broken ground.
My name can still be read in beech trees' bark,
Oenone, where your dagger left its mark;
And as those tree trunks grow, so does my name—
Grow tall and straight to advertise my claim!
There is a willow at the riverside
On which our names are carven side by side:
Long may it live, that weeping willow tree
Whose wrinkled bark displays this poetry:
"Can Paris leave Oenone? Sooner will
Xanthus reverse its course and flow uphill."
Turn backward, Xanthus! Waters, seek your source!
Paris deserted me without remorse.

My fate was sealed on that occasion—whence
Began this winter of indifference—
When naked, Venus, June, Pallas too,
Indecent stripped of armor, came to you
For judgment. Coldly, with astonishment,
I shuddered as you told of the event.
I asked our elders, so great was my fright,

And they agreed your conduct was not right.
Its timbers felled and trimmed, your well-caulked boat
Upon the sky-blue waves was soon afloat.
You wept at parting—that you can't deny.
Your new love is more scandalous than I.
You wept, and seeing that my eyes were wet,
We mingled tears in mutual regret.
No elm was ever trammeled by a vine
As your arms twined about this neck of mine.
And, ah—how many times your shipmates laughed
When you complained the wind detained your craft,
Knowing all along the wind was aft.
How many times you kissed me, who can tell?
Your tongue could hardly frame the word, "Farewell!"
Light breezes swell the shrouds that used to droop
Aloft, white water furrows at the poop:
I watch your sail until it disappears,
Drenching the sand with my unhappy tears.
I pray the sea-green Nereids to bring
You swiftly back—though I lose everything!
In answer to my prayers you have returned
With someone else. Thus is devotion spurned.

A breakwater of stone, that was a steep
Mountain, confronts the breakers of the deep:
Descrying thence your sails, I felt an urge
To hurry to you through the salt sea surge.
Glimpsing some scarlet on the foredeck while
I dithered, I flinched, for that was not your style.
Sped by the breeze, the ship drew near and docked.
Seeing a woman with you, I was shocked—
What's more—and how could I contain my pique?—

To see her clinging to you, cheek to cheek.
Indeed I beat my breast and tore my dress
And scratched my tear-drenched face in my distress,
Till holy Ida rang with my lament;
And there, to my dear rocks, in tears, I went.
May Helen mourn for your inconstancy.
One day, and feel the grief she brought on me!

Ladies who leave their husbands overseas
To follow you—now you take joy in these;
But when you led a needy shepherd's life,
Then I alone was that poor shepherd's wife.
Your wealth and palaces don't mean a thing
To me, nor my alliance to a king,
Though Priam should be willing to permit
Our marriage, and his queen acknowledge it.
I'm sure I'm worthy of a potentate;
My hands are made to hold the reins of state.
And just because I used to lie beside
You underneath a tree, do not deride
My qualifications as a royal bride.
There's safety in my love, moreover: for
My sake no ships are launched, no threats of war.
Is this the prize that pride and lust have brought,
A fugitive by warring armies sought?
Should she be given back? Go ask your brothers,
Hector, Deiphobus, and the others;
Ask Antenor and Priam, too—their age
Is great enough by now to make them sage.
A bad beginning, to prefer your lust
To your country! Such misconduct must
Make you ashamed. Her husband's cause is just.

You won't, if you are prudent, trust the charms
Of one like her who fell into your arms.
As Menelaus mourns the outrage of
His bed dishonored by a stranger's love,
So you will too. No cunning can recall
Fidelity when lost for one and all.
She burns with love for you? So loved she once
Her husband, who now sleeps alone, poor dunce.
The luck of Hector and Andromache
We might have had if you had married me.
But you are flighty as the leaves that fly
Before the fickle breezes, brittle, dry,
And no more weighty than a head of wheat
When desiccated by the summer's heat.

Your sister thus—Cassandra—prophesied,
As I recall, her toused locks untied:
"Oenone, why attempt to sow the sand?
Fruitlessly your oxen plough the strand.
A Grecian cow is coming, to undo
(Heaven forfend!) your country, home, and you.
Sink her filthy vessel if you can.
The blood with which it's fraught is Phrygian."
Her women seized her in her vatic fit;
My blond hair stood on end in awe of it.
Ah, prophetess, you proved too true, too plain:
This Grecian cow has ravaged my domain.
Though fair of face, this false adulteress
Betrayed her marriage for a guest's caress.
Some Theseus—unless I've got the name
Wrong—abducted her before you came
Along. You think that lusty youth returned

Her good as new? You wonder where I learned
This cynicism love so richly earned?
You talk of force and call her innocent?
Someone so often ravished must consent.

Yet I to my unfaithful mate am true,
Though by your rules I might be false to you.
Swift-footed satyrs rushed, a wanton rout,
Through thickets where I hid, to find me out;
From Faunus, pine boughs round his horny head,
Through soaring Ida's foothills, too, I fled.
The god that founded Troy made love to me;
Apollo took my prized virginity,
But not without a fight: I pulled his hair
And scratched him on the cheeks and everywhere.
I did not ask my price in gems and gold,
For which free bodies wickedly are sold.
Seeing my worth, he taught me medicine
Himself, the skills my hands are gifted in.
Of all medicinal herbs and roots I know
The use, wherever in the world they grow.
If only love were curable by such
Simples! My knowledge does not help me much.
Even my benefactor used to herd
Cattle, and fell in love himself, I've heard.

Relief, which earth with all her produce can't
Afford—or great Apollo—you can grant.
You can, and I deserve your kindness, for
At least I did not cause the Trojan War.
Still, once your childhood playmate, I belong
To you, and shall, I pray, my whole life long.

PARIS TO HELEN (XVI)

In this and the other paired letters (XVI–XVII, XVIII–XIX, and XX–XXI) we encounter an argument no longer one-sided, which ceases to echo with the unspoken or simply silent pathos of a prayer. To the other, dead, letters the answers are not so much implicit as unimaginable: nothing prevented Ovid from supplying the replies of Ulysses, Demophoön, and the rest but poetic tact and the rules of the genre—broken, bent, or just adapted in the case of answered letters as they would be in the ephemeral epistolary novels of the eighteenth century. The correspondence of Paris and Helen, Leander and Hero, and Acontius and Cydippe invokes and exploits the more formal rules of adversarial debate as doubtless practiced in the classrooms of Ovid's youth. Yet in these ludic trials it is worthy of remark that the accused speaks before the plaintiff does.

Of Paris enough is said not only by Oenone (II) and Helen (XVII)—and in the next note—but by himself in this letter. Beginning with his parentage in line 1, he leaves out nothing—or nothing that can redound to his supposed advantage, including his familial ties to such notorious male sex objects as Tithonus, plaything of the dawn (Aurora), and Ganymede, the original catamite. Helen in turn will answer his arguments point by point, even as to the hardly relevant details of her husband Menelaus' sanguinary descent, via Atreus and Pelops, from Tantalus, whose torment by perpetual hunger and thirst in Hades gives us a useful verb. Helen and Paris were descended in differing degrees of proximity from Jupiter (Jove, or Zeus), but then so was everybody who was anybody in those mythic days. If Paris seems to embody the masculine point of view generally slighted in the *Heroides,* he is represented here as throughout classical literature as unmanly, foppish, a drone to Helen's immortal queen bee. The heroic age,

unlike our own, despised the womanizer as effeminate. In Paris'
defense it must be said that unlike such manly men as Theseus and
Achilles, he did not desert or otherwise mistreat his ladylove.

The two lines in square brackets were supplied by the transla-
tor to fill a lacuna in the Latin text.

From Priam's son, whom nothing can avail
But Leda's daughter's salutation: hail!
Shall I speak out? Or is my love so well
Known that it would be tedious to tell?
Is my desire more obvious than I
Desire? You know that secrecy was my
Strong preference, until the day when we're
Free to enjoy each other without fear.
But I dissemble badly: who could hide
A fire whose brilliance cannot be denied?
If you insist that I articulate
The matter, *ardent* would describe my state.
Forgive my frankness, please, and read the rest
Not with a frowning face and lips compressed,
But with that air which suits your beauty best.
Your kind reception of this billet-doux
Fills me with hopes you'll treat me kindly, too,
And that the queen of love made no mistake
About this quest she bade me undertake—
For, just in case you didn't know, divine
Protection of the highest kind is mine,
And I am brought here by a god's design.

The prize is great, but no more than my due.
Venus herself has promised me to you.

She aided me to trace the mazy way
Across the broad seas from the Trojan bay,
And furnished favorable winds, for she,
Born of the sea, is mistress of the sea.
Just as she lulled the stormy waves to rest,
May she assuage the tumult in my breast
And give my hopes safe harbor as your guest.
I brought with me what I did not discover
Here: my raison d'être as a lover.
Neither by storm nor error was I brought
Hither: this was the shore my vessel sought.
Don't think I sail the seas with goods for sale
(Heaven protect my tiny capital!)
Or that as a tourist I have come
(For we have bigger towns than yours at home!).
It's you I seek, whom Venus, don't forget,
Made mine. I yearned for you before we met;
Before I saw you, my soul recognized
The face that fame at first had advertised;
Nor is it strange if Cupid's arrows are
Equally fatal when shot from afar.
So fate decreed; don't try to topple fate.
Believe the tale I faithfully relate.

While in my mother's womb I lingered too
Late, my delivery long overdue,
She dreamt that from her swollen belly came
Forth an enormous firebrand all aflame.
Hecuba leapt up terrified, and told
Her nightmare to her husband, and the old
King asked his augurs what the dream foretold.
They prophesied that I'd set Troy on fire,

(Meaning, by this incendiary desire).
[Exposed at birth, I was adopted by
Shepherds who raised me as a shepherd.] My
Good looks seemed to belie my humble birth,
My spirit, too, proclaimed my hidden worth.
In Ida's wooded vales there is a lone-
Some spot with oaks and pine trees overgrown,
Where neither placid sheep nor lazy cows
Nor goats that love a craggy landscape browse.
From there I glimpsed, when I had climbed a tree,
Beyond the walls and roofs of Troy, the sea.
Once, suddenly the earth was shaken by
Footsteps—it sounds incredible, but I
Speak truth: before my eyes on winged feet
Hermes alighted. (Let me just repeat
The things I was permitted to behold.)
His godly fingers held a wand of gold.
Then on the greensward Juno, Pallas, and
Venus appeared with dainty feet to stand.
Sheer stupefaction and dumb terror made
My hair stand on end. "Don't be afraid,
Just judge this beauty contest," Hermes said,
"Resolve these beauties' quarrel, and advise
Which of the three is worthy of first prize."
Then, Jove's command conveyed, without delay
Lest I refuse, he went his airy way.
Gradually I felt my nerve recover
Till I was not afraid to look them over.
They looked so lovely that I, to begin
With, wished that every one of them could win.
One nonetheless appealed to me above

The others—she, you know, who stirs both love
And rivalry. The bribes with which each tried
To influence the way I should decide!
Minerva courage, Juno power vaunted,
But I could not determine what I wanted,
Till Venus laughed, "Don't let such gifts affect
Your judgment, Paris. Dire is their effect.
I'll give you love. Though Leda's daughter's charms
Are unsurpassed, she'll fall into your arms."
Beauty's bribe proved irresistible,
And Venus returned to heaven invincible.

Meanwhile at last my fortunes had improved.
By certain signs my royal birth was proved;
Priam received his long-lost son with joy,
Decreeing a public holiday for Troy.
Girls yearned for me just as I yearn for you,
Thus you alone possess what not a few
Sighed for; not only dames of high degree
But dryads, even, fell in love with me,
And if to Oenone I prefer
Yourself, no paramour is worthier.
I'm bound all other women to disparage
Now that I hope to win your hand in marriage.
My imagination used to keep
Your image before me, waking or asleep.
What will your presence do, whom I desire
Unseen? I burn before I touch the fire.

Not one to harbor hopes too long in vain,
I tried my luck upon the bounding main.
First to my hatchet Asian pine trees fell,

Or any kind of wood that floated well;
The slopes of Gargara were stripped for timber,
And lofty Ida furnished me much lumber.
Curving hulls were built with oak keels, bent
And covered with a wooden tegument.
The rigging, masts and sails were added now,
And icons of the gods hung from the prow—
Venus on mine, who'd promised me a bride,
Full-length, with little Cupid at her side.
Soon all these preparations were complete,
And I could hardly wait to launch my fleet;
But, with my parents begging me to stay,
My undertaking suffered more delay.
Sister Cassandra then began to wail
Just as the ships were ready to set sail,
"Why all this rush to fetch home fire and slaughter
Worse than you can guess across the water?"
True seer! the flames she prophesied are real,
For in my heart a raging fire I feel.

So I set out, and making use of most
Favorable winds, approached the Grecian coast.
Your husband made me welcome, not without
Discreet divine encouragement, no doubt;
Undoubtedly he showed me everything
In Sparta he deemed worth exhibiting.
So keen to see your famous charms was I
That nothing else at all could catch my eye;
And when I saw you, even as I held
My breath, my heart with new emotions swelled.
The face and form of Venus when she came
To judgment, I recall, looked much the same;

Had you competed in that contest, she
Might not have won the prize so easily.
Both far and wide extends your beauty's fame:
There is no land that does not praise your name;
Your loveliness has its equivalent
Nowhere from orient to occident.
Believe me, fame depreciates your true
Beauty, and rumour almost slanders you.
I find more here than hearsay promised me;
Legend falls short of your reality.

No wonder Theseus esteemed your charms
In toto worthy of a hero's arms!
You illustrated Spartan mores when
You wrestled nude in public with nude men.
Well, who could blame him? Why return you, though?
A prize like you should never be let go.
I think that I would sooner lose my head
Than see somebody steal you from my bed;
Willingly these arms will never give
You up, or let you leave me while you live.
I'd not have sent you back before I got
Something venereal, no matter what;
You would have given me your maidenhead,
Or that which may be sacrificed instead.
But simply give yourself, and you'll discover
In Paris a completely faithful lover,
For only in the ashes of my pyre
Will my enflamed concupiscence expire.

You I preferred to those great realms with which
Jove's wife and sister promised to enrich

Me; if I could embrace you I'd despise
Minerva's promises to make me wise.
I don't regret my choice as foolish now;
My mind is made up once for all, I vow.
I beg you not to bring my hopes to nought,
Worthy of being with such trouble sought!
No base-born suitor for your noble hand
Am I; you shan't wed badly, understand.
You'll find a member of the Pleiades
And Jove himself among our family's
Forbears, and few mere mediocrities.
My father rules the Asian continent,
Infinite in resources and extent;
There countless cities, gilded domes you'll see,
And temples worthy of their deity.
The towered walls of Troy you shall behold,
Walls which Apollo's music built of old.
What can I tell you of the populace,
Who seem for earth almost too numerous?
Matrons of Troy will welcome you, for whom
The royal palace scarcely can find room.
You'll frequently exclaim, "How poor is Greece,
Whose cities have one wealthy house apiece!"

I shouldn't sneer at Sparta, though in jest:
The land that bore you I consider blest.
Yet Sparta's stingy. You deserve to dress
Richly; that spot ill suits your loveliness.
With such a face you should spare no expense
On novel and exotic ornaments.
(Seeing the getup of our men of war,
You'll wonder what the Trojan women wore!)

Come, daughter of the Spartan countryside,
Do not disdain to be a Trojan's bride.
Trojan he was, and of our royal line,
Who now dilutes the gods' ambrosial wine;
Trojan, Aurora's husband, snatched away
By the divine precursor of the day;
Trojan, Anchises, whom the mother of
The wingèd Loves on Ida loved to love.
You will not say your husband can compare
To me in youth and beauty, that I'll swear.
I do not have a relative, at least,
Who caused a blackout with his bloody feast.
Did Priam's father's bloody treachery
Give a bad name to the Myrtoan sea?
Among my ancestors, none vainly craves
For food and drink amid the Stygian waves.
Yet, notwithstanding his descent, your spouse
Can boast of Jove's connection with his house.
And every night and all night long, this cad
Embraces you. It really is too bad!

I barely see you when we meat at meal-
Times—and then what agonies I feel!
I only wish that my worse enemies
Might all partake of banquets such as these!
Seeing that boor, his arm about your bare
Shoulders, I truly wish I weren't there.
I burst with envy, watching him caress
Your lovely body underneath your dress.
In drink, when tenderly you kiss him right
In front of me, I drown the horrid sight,
Lowering my eyes if he holds you too tight.

In short, revolted by the things I saw,
The food I didn't want stuck in my craw.
Often I groaned aloud, and heard soon after
How my groans provoked your giddy laughter.
But when with wine I tried to quench desire,
Intoxication added fire to fire.
To see no more, I turned my head away,
But constantly my looks would stray your way.
The sight was painful, but what could I do?
My torment would be worse away from you.
I try to hide my state, I do my best,
But still my secret love is manifest,
Not just by word of mouth: my wounds are known
To you as well as if they were your own—
I wish that they were known to you alone!
How often tearfully I turned aside,
Lest Menelaus wonder why I cried.
Sometimes when drunk, recounting some romance,
I lent a personal significance
To every word, encountering your glance.
Who guessed that under a fictitious name
Myself and each true lover was the same?
At times, that I might speak more saucily,
I simulated inebriety.
Your dress, if it fell open, might lay bare
Your breasts, at which I could not help but stare:
Whiter than snow or milk they are, or than
Jove when he lay with Leda as a swan.
Astonished at this vision, I let slip
The goblet's twisted handle from my grip.
Each time you kissed your daughter, I would take

Your kisses from her lips for your sweet sake.
Singing old lays of love I'd sprawl supine,
Or with a nod send you a secret sign.
Your maids of honor recently I dared
Approach with winning words, but they declared
Only that they were scared, and left me there
Without an answer, halfway through my prayer.

I wish the gods would make you the reward
Of him who won your favors by the sword!
Like Atalanta, cunningly outrun,
Or Hippodameia once by Pelops won,
Like Deianira, carried off by force
By Hercules, who changed a river's course.
In such case, my bravado might succeed,
And you would know that you'd been won indeed!
But now there's nothing else for me to do
But kiss your feet, if you'll allow me to,
And press my suit respectfully with you.
Sister of the Dioscuri, your worth
Makes you their representative on earth.
Glorious beauty, who, had you not been
Jupiter's daughter, would have been his queen,
Either I'll take you home to by my wife
Or here in exile I shall end my life.
Love's arrow did not merely graze my heart
But penetrated to the deepest part;
Transfixed by that celestial dart, I guess
My sister really was a prophetess!
Helen, this fateful love do not deride,
If you would have the gods upon your side.
So we may speak more privately, invite

Me to your bedroom at the dead of night.
Are you afraid to shame your marriage bed
And to betray the royal oaf you wed?
Poor, simpleminded Helen! To believe
Your looks innocuous—that *is* naive!
Alter your face, or else become more kind:
A modest loveliness is hard to find.
Venus and Jove enjoy the furtive act—
Like that in which he fathered you, in fact.
With parentage like yours, how could you be
Chaste? Is there nothing in heredity?
Behave yourself at Troy when we get there:
I want to be your only love affair!
Sin now, our wedding day will put it right—
If Venus' promises turn out alright!

So much your husband's actions seem to say:
To give me a free hand he stays away.
No better time (he says) to visit Crete.
Oh, what a man! So prudent and discreet!
He left with this hospitable request:
"Take care for my sake of our Trojan guest."
But his commandment you neglect, I swear,
For of your guest you do not take good care.
If you think your god-given beauty can
Be rightly appreciated by that man,
You're wrong; for if he knew your value, would
He trust a stranger with his greatest good?
Even if you do not believe me, we
Should profit from such blind complicity,
Or we'd be stupider than he, to miss
A golden opportunity like this.

He all but ties the knot with his own hands,
So let's do what the simpleton demands.
Now all night long alone in bed you lie,
Night after endless night, and so do I.
Why not anticipate our honeymoon,
When night will be more radiant than noon?
I'll swear, in any formula that you
Suggest, and by your gods, that I'll be true.
If confidence is not misplaced, I hope
In person to persuade you to elope.
Afraid the deed will cover you with shame?
Well, don't be; I alone shall take the blame.
I'll merely follow Theseus' and your brothers'
Examples, as more pertinent than others';
For weren't you carried off by Theseus,
And weren't your brothers just as amorous?
The same old story will be told of us.
The Trojan fleet lies ready in the bay,
And wind and oar will speed our getaway.
You'll disembark at Troy like royalty;
The throng will hail a new divinity;
Along your route will clouds of incense rise
As at each step a sacred victim dies.
To every gift the house of Priam brings
You, Troy will add resplendent offerings.
But I can only hint at how much better
Your life will be in future, in this letter.

Don't worry, your abduction won't incite
Mayhem, with Greece arrayed in all its might.
How many women have been snatched before
Now, whose recovery provoked no war?

Believe me, Helen, there's no reason for
That fear. The Thracians were immune from slaughter
Although they took the king of Athens' daughter,
And Jason's homeland was not made to pay
When Jason with Medea ran away.
The very hero who abducted you
Once, abducted Ariadne too,
Yet Minos did not make a great to-do.
Anxiety exceeds real danger here;
We fear what we should be ashamed to fear.
But say a great war does break out: I'm tough,
My weapons are injurious enough.
The wealth of Asia, rich in men and horses,
Is more than equal to this land's resources.
Nor is your husband any braver than
Your lover, or a better fighting man.
Why, even as a lad I would attack
Our enemies to get our cattle back,
From which I got my nickname, Alexander,
Meaning "the best of men" or "the defender."
I beat the adolescent flower of Troy
In different competitions when a boy,
As an opponent formidable not
Only hand to hand, but a good shot.
You can't pretend that Menelaus ever
Struck you as precocious, skilled, and clever,
Nor can you give him what is worth another
Battalion, namely, Hector for a brother.
Do you appreciate how brave and strong
This hero is to whom you will belong?
So, either the Greeks will not create a fuss

To get you back, or they will yield to us.
I don't mind taking arms for such a wife:
Magnificent prizes do promote some strife,
And if the whole world strove for you, your name
In times to come might gain undying fame.
Don't be afraid to hope. In recompense
The gods will favor your departure hence,
So claim your just deserts with confidence.

HELEN TO PARIS (XVII)

Though certainly responsive, Helen's letter is hardly adversarial;
like Cydippe she seems primarily to be debating with herself.
Among other flimsy pretexts for rejecting him, which she has
clearly no intention of doing, she reminds Paris of her superior
birth: daughter of Zeus, disguised at the time of her conception as
a swan, and a naive or orniphile lady named Leda, Helen is sister
of the heavenly twins, or Dioscuri, Castor and Pollux, and mar-
ried to Menelaus of Sparta, scion of the bloody house of Atreus.
Eloping adulterously with Paris, she sits out the consequent war at
Troy, according to Homer, who shows her, in the *Odyssey,* at last
restored to her husband by the Greek victory, with no stain on her
character. Indeed her quasi-divine status moved more than one
poet—Stesichorus, Euripides—to swear she had never been to
Troy at all: only her eidolon, or double. Ovid's Helen, however, is
obviously packing for her Trojan trip—or her maids are—as she
pens this letter. Her earlier abduction, by Theseus, referred to
here, shows her no novice at levanting: yet her renown transcends
her reputation.

Now that your letter's thrust itself on my
Attention, politeness dictates a reply.
Profaning hospitality, you tried
To tempt your host's completely faithful bride.
Was it for this that our snug harbor gave
You shelter, tempest-tossed by wind and wave?
And though you were a total stranger, too,
Our palace portals opened wide to you?
O how could you repay our kindness so,

Intruding thus? And were you friend, or foe?
But you no doubt consider my complaint,
However justified, absurdly quaint:
Well, so be it! Better quaint than shameless,
Provided my behavior is blameless.
Although I don't affect a gloomy frown,
Sitting with knitted brows and eyes cast down,
My reputation and my pastimes are
Above reproach, and I do not, so far,
Condone adultery. I wonder at
Your confidence: what made you so sure that
I'd sleep with you? that, once a victim, I'm
Ripe for ravishment a second time?
Had he seduced me, I might feel remorse,
But how was I to counter force with force?
Yet Theseus got no pleasure from his act;
I came back scared, virginity intact.
I struggled so, that if he snatched a kiss
Or two, he got no more from me than this,
With which your lust would not have been content.
Theseus—thank god!—was different,
His self-restraint diminished his offense,
Nor did his youth prevent his penitence,
And your success would add to his regret.
How notorious can a woman get!

Still, I might be kind enough to hear
Your suit—who can object if love's sincere?
Which I doubt, although I'm not suspicious.
I can't pretend my face is not delicious,
But trust has led so many girls astray,
And your sweet talk is insincere, they say.

"Chaste wives are not exactly numerous":
But why should my name not be cited thus?
Perhaps you think the precedent of my
Mother was one I could be ruined by?
But Leda was deluded into sin:
A feathery seducer took her in.
If I succumb, it will be with my eyes
Open, my fall no "error" will disguise.
Her sin was blest, her partner was divine,
But where's the Jupiter to sanction mine?
Boast about your high descent, do you?
My family is quite distinguished too.
My father-in-law's remote forefather is
Jupiter, the grandfather of his
Father, Pelops, son of Tantalus—
But what has his descent to do with us?
Jove's my father; by a bird misled,
Credulous Leda took him to her bed.
Go tell the world about this tribe of yours,
And Priam, and your other ancestors,
Whom I respect—but you are fifth in line
From Jove, while my conception was divine.
Your empire is extensive, I admit,
But ours is not inferior to it,
Which, if more populous and richer than
Ours, is nonetheless barbarian.
Such promises your lavish letter made,
Even a goddess would, I'm sure, be swayed.
Your self is (were I tempted to transgress)
A better argument for wantonness.
If I don't keep my honor clear of stain,

It will be for your sake and not for gain.
And, though your gifts are precious to me, for
The giver's sake, your love means so much more
To me, and all the trouble that you take,
And all the miles you've voyaged for my sake.

I note your bold behavior, wretch, at table,
Dissembling just as far as I am able:
You look at me so naughtily that I
Find it difficult to meet your eye.
Sighing, you pick up the nearest cup
To me, and where I lately sipped you sup,
And neither your covert sign language nor
Your too expressive winks can I ignore,
Till, dreading lest my husband see the same,
Your blatant signals make me blush for shame.
"Nothing fazes him!" I whisper low,
And heaven only knows that this is so!
Scribbled on the tabletop in wine
I spotted your initials twined with mine;
Though I dismissed this then as poppycock,
I since have learned the meaning of such talk.
If I were going to sin, such blandishments
Might possibly exert some influence.
You have, I must admit, a pretty face,
And any girl might welcome your embrace.
Let others enjoy themselves in innocence!
My sense of married decency prevents
My sharing their amorous experience.
Learn from me how to dispense with beauty;
Abstinence from pleasure is a duty.
How many youths with your desires are wise,

Do you suppose? Do you alone have eyes?
The rest were less persistent, that is all.
You haven't got more heart: you've got more gall.

I wish you'd come in your swift vessel when
My maidenhood was sought by many men,
From whom I would have picked you at first sight—
My husband himself would overlook the slight.
Too late you've come to share preempted pleasures,
For what you hope to take, another treasures.
I might have liked to be your wife, but still
No husband holds me here against my will.
Stop using words to cause the downfall of
This tender heart which you affect to love.
Let me be faithful to my destiny—
You'll get no medal for seducing me.
Yet wasn't that the promise Venus made
When she and her sister goddesses displayed
Themselves before you in the Idaean glade?
One offered power, another martial pride,
But, "Helen," said the third, "will be your bride."
I can't believe those heavenly bodies lent
Their loveliness to your arbitrament,
But if they did, it surely is a lie
That your reward, and Venus' bribe, was I.
I am not so conceited I believe
Myself the greatest boon she could conceive.
Enough that men approve the way I look—
The praise of Venus only brings bad luck.
I shan't repudiate your homage, though:
How could I question what I wish were so?
If I was slow to credit you, I'm sorry:

In vital matters trust is dilatory.
I'm glad if what found favor in the eyes
Of Venus seems to you a worthy prize.
My beauty she had only to describe
And you rejected every other bribe,
So I'm your honor and your kingdom too.
I must be iron not to care for you.

Well, iron I'm not, and yet I think it wrong
To love someone to whom I can't belong.
Why should I try to till the seashore and
Pin false hopes upon the sterile sand?
Heaven knows that I am not so clever
As to deceive my doting husband ever!
In writing this clandestine letter, I'm
Abusing the alphabet for the first time.
Happy the skilled adulteress! I guess
How tricky are the paths of wickedness.
Confused, tormented by anxiety,
I think that every eye is fixed on me—
With reason: tittle-tattle I have heard,
Low talk, of which my handmaid brings me word.
Dissemble—or perhaps you'd rather go
Home? Why go, when you dissemble so?
In Menelaus' absence be discreet;
Our freedom is enlarged but not complete.
My husband was called suddenly away
On urgent business brooking no delay—
At least I thought it urgent anyway,
And when he stalled encouraged him to pack:
"The sooner you leave, the sooner you'll get back."
Reassured, he left with one request:

"Take care of Sparta—and our Trojan guest."
I had to laugh, and struggling to repress
My ribald giggles, answered merely, "Yes."
But now he's gone off on this Cretan jaunt
Don't think you can do anything you want,
For though he's absent I can feel his eyes
On us—have you forgotten kings have spies?
Rumor aggravating our position,
Your constant praise confirms his worst suspicion.
Renown, however pleasant, will be my
Ruin; better to give fame the lie.
You think it odd he leaves you with his wife?
He trusts my conduct and my blameless life.
He thinks that he can count, although my beauty
Makes him nervous, on my sense of duty.
"Do not overlook," you're telling me,
"This heaven-given opportunity
To profit by such dumb complacency."
Your opposition tempts me, but I'm scared;
I can't decide, my mind is unprepared.
My husband's gone, and you are lonely too,
Your looks please me as much as mine please you;
Long nights in the same house, and your discourse
Too sweet for purely verbal intercourse—
Everything is tempting me to stray,
Only some secret scruple blocks my way.

Where persuasion failed, may force succeed!
The only cure for backwardness indeed!
Victims sometimes don't find rape so bad:
I wish someone would force me to be glad.
It's easier to quell a new desire;

A little water quenches a fresh fire.
No stranger's love can be depended on;
Just when you think it's here to stay, it's gone.
Hypsipyle and Ariadne were
Each tricked into sleeping with a traveler,
And did you not quite cavalierly wrong
Poor Oenone whom you liked so long?
You can't deny it! I have studied, so
To find out all about you, don't you know.
You could not, if you wanted, keep your word,
For your departure cannot be deferred.
Even as you're talking to me, and
While our night of bliss is being planned,
A western wind will waft you to your land;
Yes, in the midst of our debaucheries
You'll leave, and love will vanish on the breeze.
Shall I come too, as you are urging me
To do, your celebrated Troy to see
And marry into Priam's family?
No, am I so indifferent to fame
That I should fill the world with my bad name?
How will Sparta, how will Greece react?
And all of Asia—Troy itself, in fact?
What will Priam think, and Hecuba,
And all your brothers and your sisters-in-law?
How can you ever think me innocent
Again when you provide this precedent?
Every chance newcomer to appear
In Troy will fill you with dismay and fear;
Often in anger will you call me whore
While your own fault you're willing to ignore,

At once the scourge and prompter of my crime.
I pray that I'll be dead before that time!
And yet the splendid opulence of Troy,
Surpassing all you promised, I'd enjoy,
Purple and precious raiment, gold of which
There would be heaps enough to make me rich.

Forgive me, but your gifts are not so grand.
Something still keeps me in my native land.
What help, if on your coast I should be wrecked,
From brother or father could I then expect?
Although false-hearted Jason promised all
She wanted to Medea, after all
Wasn't she driven from his father's hall?
How could she return, so much maligned,
To the family she left behind?
I'm not afraid—nor was her ladyship,
But between cup and lip there's many a slip,
And many a ship with which the waves make sport,
You'll find, that had no trouble leaving port.
That bloody brand alarms me, which before
Your birth was due your mother dreamt she bore,
That prophecy as well, that Greece will come
And fire the topless towers of Ilium.
Of course you're Venus' favorite, for she
Owes to you a twofold victory:
I fear the losing pair whom, if your boast
Is true, you robbed of what they wanted most.
No doubt if I eloped with you, a war
Would follow. Is our love worth fighting for?
Did not Hippodamia incite
The centaurs and the Lapiths once to fight?

And do you think the justice of their cause
Will for a moment give my menfolk pause?
Although you vaunt your valor to the skies,
Such boastful words your countenance belies.
Your face and form are better fashioned for
Venus than Mars; her service suits you more;
Let strong men fight, while you make love not war.
Ask Hector, whom you laud, to fight for you:
Other fields deserve your derring-do,
And there I'd join you, were I not afraid,
And so would any knowledgeable maid.
Perhaps I shall, my honor laid aside,
And offer you my hands, which time has tied.
As for that tête-à-tête, I know what kind
Of private interview you have in mind!
Not so fast—your plans are immature
As yet—but time is on your side, I'm sure.
It's time that this clandestine letter, penned
With furtive, flagging fingers, had an end.
Further communication will be through
My maids, companions, and advisers too.

LAODAMIA TO PROTESILAUS (XIII)

Laodamia's situation recalls that of many a Roman matron, such as Octavia's long and finally futile wait for Mark Antony. With nothing but a simulacrum to fall back on, her patience would not be rewarded like Penelope's (I). Protesilaus seems one of those men whose whole existence culminates in a single act—in his case, leaping first ashore at Troy, and thus with his precipitate death earning five lines in Homer's *Iliad* (II, 698–702), one sure guarantee of undying fame. The delay at Aulis to which Laodamia refers, the subject of a play by Euripides, was occasioned by Agamemnon's hesitation to sacrifice his daughter Iphigenia for fair weather.

> Your wife sends her best wishes, with her love,
> From Thessaly which you are master of.
> The wind keeps you at Aulis, so they say:
> Where was that wind the day you stole away?
> Why then did not high waves impede your flight?
> That was the time for stormy seas, all right!
> Giving you kisses and advice galore,
> I wished that there were time to tell you more.
> You were whisked off precipitately by
> A wind that sailors fancy but not I;
> The wind that favors sailors lovers fear.
> So I was torn from your embraces, dear,
> My parting words unfinished on the air,
> Unable to complete my final "Fare-
> Well," before the north wind fell upon
> Your sails, and in a twinkling you were gone.

Happy as long as you remained in view,
I gladly strained my eyes to follow you
Until I couldn't make you out for sure,
And then your sails became my cynosure;
At last across the vacant sea I peered
Where you and your fleet sails had disappeared.
Then all the lights went out and darkness rolled
Across my eyes; exhausted, sick, and cold,
I collapsed on bended knees, I'm told,
At length resuscitated by cold water
With which my grieving parents drenched their daughter—
A pointless act, though kind, for I resent
Not being left to die of discontent.
With consciousness my suffering returned;
With licit love my matronly heart burned.
I don't care if my coiffure is a mess,
And am indifferent to how I dress;
Hither and yon, as madness prompts, like one
Touched by Bacchus' magic wand, I run.
The local women throng to remonstrate,
"Laodamia, don your robes of state!"
Shall I my gold and purple silks deploy
While you wage war beneath the walls of Troy?
I think of your helmet when I comb my hair
And, dressing, of the armor you must wear.

I'd like by my dishevelment to share
Your hardships, and in mourning spend the war.
Paris' good looks engendered bad luck for
His kin. I hope he proves less of a pest
On the battlefield than as a guest.

If only he'd found fault with Helen's face
Or she had thought his own less full of grace!
How Menelaus strove for what he'd lost,
And what a flood of tears his vengeance cost!
All such calamaties, O Gods, avert,
And bring my husband home to me unhurt.
Thoughts of this wretched war make my tears flow
As copious and fast as melting snow.
Ida, Troy, Simois—when I hear
These names, the very sound fills me with fear.
Would Paris have dared elope with her, unless
Prepared to fight? He knew his strength, I guess.
Splendid in gold he came to the attack
With all the wealth of Asia on his back,
Backed by an expeditionary force
And all Troy's almost infinite resource.
Was Helen overwhelmed by that display,
Obnoxious to the Greeks? Well, so they say.
Of Hector—what's his name?—I'm frightened, for
Paris described him as a god of war:
Beware of him, whoever he may be,
And, if you still care anything for me,
Impress that name upon your memory.
Eluding him, remember to beware
Of others: there are many Hectors there;
And when you arm yourself, think of your wife:
The life you save—your own—may be her life.
Why shouldn't Troy succumb before the armed
Might of Greece—so long as you're unharmed?
Let Menelaus fight in the front line,
Fit place for Helen's husband but not mine.

Your duty's different: strive but to survive,
And come back to my loving arms alive.
O Trojans, from so many, spare one foe,
I pray, lest from his wound my lifeblood flow.
He's not the type in savage hand-to-hand
Combat to risk his life, you understand;
Love, not war, he is past master of:
Let others fight; let Protesilaus love.

I wished to call you back; keen as I was,
I tell you, superstition gave me pause.
Ominously, when you were leaving for
Troy, you tripped as you went out the door;
I said to myself immediately, "May
This augur my husband's safe return, I pray."
Lest you should be too rash I tell you this;
Now try my foolish fancies to dismiss.
That Greek who first sets foot—I don't know whom—
Upon the soil of Troy shall meet his doom.
I pity the widow first to mourn her mate
And pray you prove not too precipitate,
But of the thousand ships, let your ship be
The thousandth and last to crease the well-worn sea,
And, furthermore, see you're the last to land;
Take your time—it's not your native strand.
Return full speed ahead, until you reach
Home and run your keel up on the beach.
While Phoebus climbs on high or sinks from sight,
You visit me with sorrow day and night,
But more by night than day, for night has charms
For young wives cuddled in somebody's arms.
I chase delusive dreams in my chaste bed,

And, lacking real joys, enjoy false ones instead.
But why before me does your pale ghost stand,
Uttering moans I cannot understand?
Awaking, I placate the gods of hell,
Feeding their altars frankincense as well
As tears, at which libation the flames shine
Brighter, as if I sprinkled them with wine.
When shall my loving arms hold you again
Until I swoon with happiness? and when,
United in our double bed once more
You tell me all about your splendid war,
Shall I listen fascinated, yet
Giving as many kisses as I get,
Till, interrupted by such sweet applause,
Your tongue grows livelier with every pause?
But as I think of Troy, and wind and wave,
My courage fails, and hope is not so brave.
Even the news, that weather may delay
The expedition, fills me with dismay:
You're making preparations anyway.
Some strive in vain to reach their native shores;
You risk your life to get away from yours.
Neptune smooths no highway through the foam
To Troy, his favorite city. Greeks, go home!
Where do you think you're headed? Listen to
The contrary winds that are obstructing you:
This holdup is no sudden accident
But seems to indicate divine intent.
And what's this war about? A filthy whore!
Then let the fleet of Greece turn back before
It is too late. But what have I just said?

Recalling you's like calling back the dead.
Better wish you bon voyage instead!

I envy Trojan women, who can cry
Over their menfolk with the foe nearby,
The bride who herself may help her husband don
His armor and put his Trojan helmet on
And, arming him for battle, steal a kiss—
Both a duty and a pleasure, this—
Bidding him return and bring back these
Weapons to the god of victories.
Keeping her warning fresh in mind, he'll fight
Cautiously: he has his home in sight.
His wife when he returns will then divest
Her hero of helmet, shield, and all the rest,
And take his weary body to her breast.
We doubt and fear, we Grecian wives, and know
That everything that can occur does so.
While you're campaigning in that far-off place
I keep a waxen image of your face
On which I lavish the endearments due
You, and blandishments and kisses, too.
It is not a mere effigy, like some:
You'd swear it was yourself, were it not dumb.
I gaze at it, and pressing it to my
Bosom in place of my real husband, I
Whisper, as if the waxwork could reply,
"I swear by all that I hold sacred, your
Safe return, the body I adore,
And by the equal incandescence of
Passionate desire and married love,
And your dear head, which I desire to see

Come home unscathed and grow gray gracefully,
I'll follow you wherever you are led
Alive or—alas! the thought fills me with dread."
So my last letter ends with this short prayer:
If you still care for me, my love, take care!

BRISEIS TO ACHILLES (III)

To tell in full the story of Briseis, brief as it is, would be to epitomize the *Iliad,* for she furnished the occasion of Achilles' wrath, the real subject of that poem. Furthermore, all that we know about her is from Homer and his commentators, who portray her as the daughter of one Briseus of Lyrnessus, an obscure town of the Troad which Achilles sacks along the way; though the names of her scrappy brothers are nowhere recorded, she is said to be the widow of somebody called Mynes, for what that is worth. Achilles' captive and concubine, she was taken from him by Agamemnon, commander of the expedition to Troy, in compensation for his own prize, Chryseis, whom he was forced to surrender in book 1. Later, sulking in his tent, Achilles will not have Briseis back at any price, and threatens to decamp. The death of his best friend, Patroclus, while fighting in Achilles' own armor, changes his mind; and it is over Patroclus' body that Briseis is last heard lamenting, in book XIX.

This letter, scrawled in my barbaric hand,
Though Greek, perhaps you cannot understand?
The blots you see were made by tears, but each
Teardrop possesses all the weight of speech.
If grumbling at one's master be no sin,
With you as man and master I'll begin.
It's not your fault that I was traded to
Your rival on demand—yet it was too!
You gave me up without a struggle when
I was demanded by his servingmen,
Who traded looks, as if without a word

To ask, where was this love of which they'd heard?
You could have stalled. My pain would brook delay,
I did not kiss you when I went away,
But wept and tore my hair incessantly,
Unhappy at my new captivity.
Bent on returning when I saw a chance,
I feared my keeper's hostile vigilance;
If I slipped out at night I was afraid
I'd end up as a Trojan lady's maid.
Delivered up because that was my fate,
Night after night I wait. You hesitate
To rescue me. It soon will be too late.
Even Patroclus whispered in my ear
When I was handed over, "Have no fear,
Before you know it you will be back here."
Not seeking me is one thing: was it quite
Civil to resist with all your might?

Phoenix and Ajax came to see you, one
Your comrade, one your father's brother's son—
Ulysses, too, to yield me up. Their pleas
Enhanced the worth of splendid gifts like these:
Twenty cauldrons of superb design,
And seven brazen tripods just as fine,
Ten gold talents, and twelve horses in
Addition, of the kind that always win;
And, though you hardly need them, furthermore,
Some lovely girls from Lesbos, spoils of war;
And one of Agamemnon's daughters three
To wife—an ostentatious luxury.
The bribe you should have paid out for my sake,
When it was offered, you refused to take.

What fault has made me worthless in your eyes?
Our flighty love, how fast and far it flies
So soon! Does bad luck dog the steps of sorrow,
And shall I see no happier tomorrow?

I saw your martial fury tear apart
The town in which I played no common part;
I saw how my adored three brothers fell,
One in blood and bloody death as well;
I saw my husband stretched out in the mud
Which he ensanguined with his entrails' blood;
When I'd lost everything, what could I do
But find a sort of substitute in you,
My master, husband, and dear brother too?
Upon your mother's sacred name you swore
I was in luck—a prisoner of war!
Of course you may reject me, though I've got
A dowry of sorts—Achilles can't be bought!
Now rumor goes that when the sky grows pale,
The weather notwithstanding, you will sail.
When I got wind of this new wickedness,
My poor heart skipped a beat in its distress.
Whom will you cede me to when you depart,
You heartless brute, to mend my broken heart?
I pray to be consumed by lightning or
Swallowed by the gaping earth before,
Forsaken, I will watch the wake of foam
Behind your ships as they set sail for home.
But if homesickness calls you back, my lord,
I won't take up a lot of room on board;
I'll travel as a captive, not a bride;
I have some skill in fancywork beside.

Your wife will be the pick of Grecian wives—
At least I hope so, and I hope she thrives
As Jove's great-granddaughter-in-law, and one
Whom Nereus would choose for his grandson;
While I, a lowly spinster, shall diminish
The wool allotted me, but never finish.
But do not let your wife torment me: she
Will find some way to be unkind to me.
Don't let my hair be shorn in front of you,
Blithely remarking, "Yes, I had her, too!"
Yet rather that than be abandoned here
Despised, alas! That is my greatest fear.

What more do you want, now Agamemnon's pique
Abates and you're implored by every Greek
In tears? In all things else victorious
Conquer yourself and be magnanimous!
Why should that bully Hector hector us?
Take arms, Achilles—but first take me back,
And, blest by Mars, return to the attack.
For my sake cease your sulks, and as I've been
Its cause, let me alleviate your spleen.
Do not suppose it foul disgrace to yield
To pressure. Meleager, when appealed
To by his wife, agreed to take the field.
You know the tale as well as I: a mother's
Curse condemned the son who slew her brothers;
Sole hope in wartime, he quit fighting, and
Stiff-necked, refused to aid his fatherland.
Only his wife could move him. Happy she!
My words are never taken seriously.
Yet I don't mind. No wifely role was mine

As my master's favorite concubine.
Called mistress by a fellow captive, my
Servile pride was ridiculed thereby.
Moreover, on my husband's grave I swear—
If he has one!—and the love I bear
My three stout-hearted, godlike brothers who
Died for their country—yes, and with it, too!
And by our love as we lay side by side,
And by your sword by which my kinsmen died:
No Mycenean ever shared my bed.
If I am lying, cast me off for dead.

But if I bade you swear that you had got
No joy from life without me, you could not.
The Greeks think you are brooding, while you rest,
Strumming your lyre, on some soft female breast.
If someone asks you why you will not fight,
You answer, "Fighting's dangerous, I might
Get hurt! In love and music I delight.
Safer by far to loll in bed with some
Sweet girl while on the Thracian lyre I strum
Than to juggle shield and lance, and wear
A heavy helmet mussing up my hair."
Once fame meant more to you than soft repose
And victory in battle. I suppose
You only fought for me? My city fell,
And all of your ambition died as well.
The gods forbid! Shake that strong spear which you
Received from Pallas, run great Hector through!
Make me your envoy, Greeks, and I'll beseech
My lord, with kisses larding my set speech.
More than Phoenix, more than Ajax I'll

Accomplish, more than all Ulysses' guile.
First I'll fold you in a fond embrace,
And hold you close and gaze into your face;
Though harsher than your mother's element,
The sea, before my silent tears relent.
You hope to see your son become a man,
Don't you, your father live out his life's span?
Likewise have pity on Briseis, please
Don't let your coldness kill me by degrees.

But since you seem so sick and tired of
Me, better death than life without your love.
Your conduct's killing me; I'm thin and wan.
Yet you're my only hope. When that is gone
I'll join the dear departed in the grave.
Condemn a woman—isn't that a brave
Gesture! Why not yourself perform the deed,
Cut my heart out and see how I bleed?
The very sword which Pallas turned aside
From Agamemnon, plunge into my side.
But no! This life, which you spared once before
When you and I were enemies, restore
Now for the sake of friendship, I implore.
Troy has victims worthier of you: go
Find your proper prey among the foe.
Whether you plan to sail or mean to stay,
Command me in your old high-handed way.

HERMIONE TO ORESTES (VIII)

Daughter of Menelaus and Helen, Hermione was originally be-
trothed to her cousin Orestes, son of Agamemnon and Clytem-
nestra, but was carried off by Pyrrhus (Neoptolemus), son of
Achilles, at least according to this version, sometime after the fall
of Troy. Accounts vary, but in most she is eventually restored to
Orestes, who at the time of writing is a fugitive from the Furies as
a result of the murder of his mother in revenge for her slaying of
his father.

> Achilles' son, as spirited as he,
> Holds me against my will, outrageously.
> I spurned him resolutely as I could
> But feminine resistance does no good.
> "What are you doing, brute?" I said, "You thought
> Me quite without protection, but I'm not."
> Deaf as the sea, he dragged me by the hair,
> While I called out, "Orestes!" to his lair.
> If Sparta fell, enslaved I would endure
> No worse at barbarian hands, I'm sure;
> In victory the Greeks did not mistreat
> Andromache so, after Troy's defeat.
>
> Orestes, if you're moved by my sad plight,
> Fearlessly assert your legal right;
> If someone stole your cattle you would take
> Arms—why dally when your wife's at stake?
> For instance, Menelaus sought his wife . . .
> Else she'd have stayed with Paris all her life.

No need to launch a thousand ships and some
Expeditionary force—just come!
I'm worthy enough of being rescued thus:
A husband's rights are worth a little fuss.
We are so closely linked to one another,
Were we not wed I'd love you like a brother.
As sister and wife I have a double claim
To your protection under either name.
My grandfather, Tyndareus, gave you me—
His age allowed him that authority;
And though, unknowing, father pledged my hand
To Pyrrhus, our engagement does still stand.
In wedding you, what mischief could I do?
By wedding him, I'd be untrue to you.
My father, Menelaus, will pardon our
Love: he too succumbed to Cupid's power,
And having been in love, he must consent—
There's my beloved mother's precedent.
As he to her, you are to me: the way
That Paris acted, Pyrrhus acts today.
Though in his father's deeds he takes such pride,
Your father's stature cannot be denied.
Agamemnon ruled the army and
Achilles too, a private in that band
Of which your father had supreme command.
Including Tantalus and Pelops, were
You only five removes from Jupiter?

No, you don't lack courage! though your deed
Was violent, your father's ghost decreed
Acts I could wish more worthy of applause,
But, forced to act, you did not choose your cause.

You did your duty, still. Aegisthus' gore,
When you dispatched him, stained the palace floor
Exactly as your father's had before.
Pyrrhus sneers at you to me, by shame
Unmoved, perverting praise of you to blame.
My face reflects the tumult of my brain;
I burst with fires my breast cannot contain.
While he maligns Orestes must I stand
By helpless with no trusty sword to hand?
Weep I may, and inundate my breast
With tears enough to lull my wrath to rest.
Of tears I have perpetual supply;
The springs that streak my cheeks run never dry.

The family curse, which I cannot escape,
Appears to make our women ripe for rape.
I'll not retail that swan's seductive lies
Nor carp at Zeus's feathery disguise.
Across the narrow isthmus Pelops brought
Hippodamia in his chariot.
Her brothers Castor and Pollux rescued my
Mother from Theseus, but by-and-by
Helen, abducted by her Trojan guest,
Had armed all Greece to serve her interest.
I can recall, but only just, the tears
Of everyone, and all their nervous fears:
Grandfather and Phoebe wept, and the twin brothers,
And Leda prayed to Jupiter and others,
And I, who'd hardly outgrown infancy,
Cried, "Mother, are you leaving without me?"
Then, when you left, lest anyone should say
I wasn't Helen's daughter, I fell prey

To Pyrrhus while my husband was away.
If only he'd escaped Apollo's bow
Achilles would condemn his son, I know.
He'd hate to see, as he did all his life,
A husband weeping for his ravished wife.
What crime of mine has called down heaven's curse?
Poor me, to whom the stars are so adverse!
I was twice orphaned, though my parents were
Alive: she left, he went to fight for her.

My babytalk did not delight your ears,
Mother, in those lonely early years,
No, never did my tiny arms embrace
Your neck, nor was your lap my resting place.
You did not bring me up, you didn't care,
And when I wed, of course you were not there.
When you returned, imagine my surprise:
My mother's face I did not recognize.
That Helen was most beautiful I knew:
Your child's identity eluded you.

No, nothing but my marriage turned out right—
And that is lost if you refuse to fight.
My father has come back, victorious,
Yet Pyrrhus holds me captive—curious
How little victory has done for us!
When Phoebus' steeds ascend the firmament
I can, though wretched, bear my discontent;
But when night locks me in my room, I lie
Upon my bitter bed and sob and sigh,
Tearful and sleepless, shunning when I can
The hateful advances of that horrid man.

Yet sometimes I forgot, and stupefied
By grief, I touched the body at my side,
Then realizing what I'd done, recoiled
As if I thought my fingers had been soiled.
Often instead of his your name slipped out:
A loving and auspicious slip, no doubt!

By our unhappy family and its sire—
Land and sea and heaven fear his ire!
And by your father's bones at last at peace
Avenged by your heroics, I, his niece,
Swear prematurely to cut short my life
If I cannot remain my cousin's wife.

PHYLLIS TO DEMOPHOÖN (II)

Son of Theseus and Phaedra, Demophoön on his way home from
Troy put in at Thrace, the eastern coast of the Balkans. There
Phyllis, daughter of King Lycurgus, went through a form of mar-
riage with him. Summoned home by news from Athens, he prom-
ised to return; but she, impatient at his tarrying, hanged herself,
and according to some fabulists became an almond tree, which
blossomed when Demophoön, belatedly returning, embraced it.
This is only one of several suicide notes among these dead let-
ters—a form at which Ovid obviously excelled.

I, your Thracian hostess, Phyllis, grieve,
Demophoön, you've overstayed your leave.
For when the hornèd moon was full once more
You promised to drop anchor off our shore;
Four times the moon has waxed and waned, with no
Sign of any Attic ship I know.
If you keep track of time as lovers do,
You'll grant that this reproach is overdue.
Hope dragged its feet, for slow is our belief
In that which, once believed, brings no relief:
Reluctantly at last love comes to grief.
For your sake I invented many lies,
Like: you were kept in port by stormy skies.
Theseus I cursed, for forcing you to stay,
Although he wasn't standing in your way.
I feared lest in the Hebrus' shoals your boat
Amid the whitecaps could not keep afloat.
How often, wretch, for your welfare I prayed,

How many incensed offerings I made!
And told myself, when wind and tide seemed quite
Favorable, "He'll come if he's all right."
Love, faithful and ingenious, discovers
Reasons enough for the delays of lovers.
Yet still you delay, contrary to divine
Mandate, unmoved by any love of mine.
My dear, your words are idle as your sails:
It isn't the wind but your good faith that fails.

Granted I love not wisely but too well:
Did I not thus deserve your love, pray tell?
I welcomed you with open arms, a crime
That only seemed a kindness at the time.
Where is the faith we swore we would maintain?
The god whose name we mostly took in vain?
Where is that promise binding you to me
For years to come, our marriage warranty?
By the sea you swore, by wind and wave
Which you had braved, and meant again to brave,
And your forefather—if he's not a myth—
Who can allay the raging deep forthwith,
And Venus whose attacks afflict me so,
Whether she wields the bow or the flambeaux,
By Juno, patroness of wedding nights,
And by Demeter's secret, mystic rites.
You never shall, should all those gods resent
Your perjuries, serve out your punishment.
Yet I was mad enough to make your ship
More seaworthy for giving me the slip,
Providing a crew to aid your escapade:
The wounds I suffer, my own weapons made!

Your lavish blandishments inspired my credence,
Your family and famous antecedents,
Even your tears. Can tears acquire such skill
At false pretenses as to flow at will?
I trusted your gods! Where's all your sweet talk now?
You could have snared me with a single vow.
Never mind I furnished you a port—
That should have been the end of my support;
My hospitality should have stopped short
Of welcoming you too warmly, like a bride,
And lying with you wrongly side by side.
I wish I had expired the night before—
Then would Phyllis not have died a whore!
I hoped for and deserved a whole lot more,
In my opinion: all great expectation
Is justified in our own estimation.

Deceiving a credulous and innocent
Girl's no glorious accomplishment:
My naivety might have made you relent!
So your palaver fooled a love-struck dame!
Your loving words procured a princess' shame—
God grant that that's your only claim to fame!
May they erect your statue in the square
At Athens, with your great ancestors' there,
Facing your famous father's, where one reads
Inscribed accounts of his heroic deeds.
Next to Scyron, Sinis, terrible
Procrustes, and the hybrid human bull,
Thebes conquered and the centaurs put to flight,
And Theseus' visit to the realms of night,
Let this be inscribed upon your statue: "He

Abused his mistress' hospitality."
The only act of his you kept in mind
Was how he left that Cretan girl behind.
His sole regret you deem his only merit;
It is your father's crime you would inherit.
But lucky Ariadne found a far
Better mate, and rides on Bacchus' car.

No wonder my spurned Thracian suitors shun
The match, since I preferred a foreign one:
"Let her go to Athens! In her place
Someone else will govern warlike Thrace."
Ends justify means? Confound him who pretends
That means are ever justified by ends!
Still, if your vessel ever hove in sight
The Thracians would admit that I was right.
I wasn't, though, nor shall I entertain
You here, or wash your weary limbs again.
The scene at parting still afflicts my heart:
Your ships in harbor, anxious to depart,
You dared to hang about my neck, and press
Your lips to mine in one long, last caress,
And mingling your tears with mine, dared to bewail
The breeze that would permit your setting sail.
These last words you spoke, and then were gone:
"Phyllis, do wait for your Demophoön."
Wait? For one whom I shall never see
Again, and watch the unforthcoming sea?
Well, I shall wait. Return some day, so you
Prove only temporarily untrue.
What do I ask in my unhappiness?
Another's arms are holding you, no less

Than Love, which brought me nothing but distress.
You left me and at once forgot my name.
"Phyllis who?" you asked, and whence she came.
Who showed you hospitality in Thrace
When worn with wandering from place to place?
Whose wealth replenished your depleted store?
I gave you much, and meant to give you more,
Even my father's kingdom, this vast land
Of Thrace, unsuited to a woman's hand,
Where shady Haemon rises to the snows
Of Rhodope, and sacred Hebrus flows.
To you I sacrificed my maidenhead
That inauspicious day when we were wed,
And your deceit defiled the marriage bed.
The furies were my bridesmaids, whose loud howls
Drowned out the mournful hymns of lonesome owls;
They all attended, wreathed in serpents, and
Brandishing a funerary brand.

But still I pace the cliffs and windswept shore,
The sea's wide panorama spread before
My eyes, both in the middle of the day,
When soil is softened by the heat of day,
And under the cold stars, I mark which way
The wind is blowing. Eagerly I hail
As heaven-sent each tiny, far-off sail.
I rush to the water's edge, and where the salt
Sea hurls its highest wave I hardly halt;
The nearer draw the ships, I faint and fail,
And would, but for my serving women, fall.
There is a gently curving bay with high
Rugged cliffs on either side, whence I

Thought I should throw myself into the sea—
And shall, since you persist in treachery!
I wish my body, carried by the tide,
Could show you an unburied suicide!
Harder than iron, or your heart, you'd say,
"Why, Phyllis, do you follow me this way?"
Sometimes I thirst for poison, then I feel
A deadly appetite for bloodstained steel;
This neck you wound your arms round to seduce
Me once would look much better in a noose.
Let timely death wipe out a tender wrong;
The means of death will not detain me long.
And for my fate my epitaph will blame
You publicly, in other words, by name:
Demophoön, though Phyllis' lover and
Her guest, procured her ruin. Understand:
His was the fault; she died by her own hand.

PENELOPE TO ULYSSES (I)

The faithful homebody par excellence, Penelope awaited Ulysses (Odysseus) not only through the Trojan War but also during his prolonged, involuntary wanderings round the Mediterranean on his way home. In the sophisticated narrative art of Homer the *Odyssey*, which with reason has been called the first novel, is almost as much Penelope's story as Odysseus'. To keep at bay her importunate suitors, Penelope attaches her choice of one of them to the completion of a piece of weaving, which she unpicks at night. Her son, and Ulysses', Telemachus—who though called a boy (*puer*) here must by now be nearly twenty, as circumstances date this letter from the year of Ulysses' return—goes abroad in search of news of his father. Odysseus' eventual return and the slaughter of the suitors provide a happy ending almost unique in the *Heroides*.

Dear husband, now you've gone so long astray,
Do not reply, but come back straightaway.
Yes, Troy has fallen—we desired its fall:
Were Priam and his city worth it all?
If only pretty Paris, making for
Sparta, had foundered in the surf offshore,
I shouldn't frigid and forsaken lie
Complaining how the dreary days drag by,
Nor would this endless web wear out my strength
As, widowed, I beguile night's weary length.
Always my fears outran reality;
Love is a thing that brings anxiety.
Dreaming bloodthirsty Trojans overcame

You, time and again I paled at Hector's name.
Did someone say he'd slain Antilochus?
The merest rumor made me timorous.
Patroclus dead while armored in deceit?
I wept that subterfuge could meet defeat.
Tlepolemus' blood imbued the Lycian spear?
His death served only to renew my fear.
My loving heart, whenever I was told
That one of you had perished, grew ice-cold.
Yet providence rewarded a chaste wife;
The sack of Troy preserved my husband's life.

See smoking altars greet our chiefs' return;
Our gods have got outlandish spoils to burn.
Brides bring oblations for their mens' salvation
Who vaunt their triumph and Troy's ruination;
Old codgers gape, girls listen all aflutter,
Wives hang on every word their husbands utter.
On tabletops they draw the battle line,
Writing the *Iliad* in a drop of wine:
"Here's Simois, there's Sigeia, and
Here did old Priam's lofty palace stand.
Achilles' tent was there, Ulysses' here,
Slain Hector's steeds stampeded there in fear . . ."
This Nestor told Telemachus when he
Set out to seek you, and our son told me:
Of Rhesus' death and Dolon's murder—while
One was undone by sleep, one died by guile—
When far too careless of your loved ones' plight
You dared slip through the Trojan lines by night,
Slaughtering many men with but one man's
Help. Did thoughts of me affect your plans?

I trembled till I heard of your success:
Back safe, and with the Trojan team, no less!
But what's the use, though you had overthrown
And razed the walls of Ilium alone,
When I'm stuck here in pseudo-widowhood
Forever, as if Ilium still stood?
For others Ilium is history,
But it remains a battlefield to me,
Although the victor tills the conquered land
With captured cattle, and the ripe crops stand
Ready to harvest where Troy stood before,
The rich soil fertilized by Trojan gore:
Half-buried bones are turned up by the plough,
And weeds grow over ruined houses now.
Heartless in victory, you tarry so
It seems that I am not allowed to know
Your whereabouts, or why you are so slow?

Every mariner repairing to
Ithaca I ask for news of you,
Giving him a letter just in case
He should encounter you by chance someplace.
I sent to Pylos, Nestor's territory:
Pylos returned a vague, confusing story.
I sent to Sparta: Sparta could not say
Through what strange lands you dawdled on your way.
I wish the Trojan ramparts were still standing
(My former imprecations notwithstanding):
I'd know where you were fighting then, and dread
Nothing worse than war, the tears I shed
Not unique, but commonplace instead.
My terror is pervasive and perverse,

Its subject matter, the whole universe.
I take all perils met on land or sea
As explanation of your truancy;
But while I fondly fret, your heart perchance
Is captivated by some stray romance?
Must I suppose you tell your beautiful
Mistress what a frump your dutiful
Wife is, only good for spinning wool?
I hope I'm wrong. Intolerable thought
That you are free to come home and will not!
And now my father wants me to divorce
You for desertion—civilly, of course.
Let him nag! I'm yours, for all her life
Penelope shall be Ulysses' wife.

Soon soothed by my submissive dedication
My father moderates his indignation.
Suitors are gathering from everywhere
To overrun your Ithaca, for there
Is none to stop this rabble wantonly
Adding my insult to your injury—
That riffraff that you entertain in your
Culpable absence from your hard-won store.
The beggar at your gate, your goatherd, too,
Disgracefully conspire to ruin you.
We three make up this unarmed garrison:
Weak wife, old father, adolescent son.
Telemachus the suitors tried to kill
When he prepared to leave against their will.
(I pray that in due course it please divine
Providence he'll close your eyes and mine!)
Besides your nanny, we're supported by

The cowman and the man who cleans the sty.
Your feeble father futilely resists
The wickedness of these extortionists,
Nor am I strong enough to route our foes.
Come quickly, our sole refuge and repose!
You have a son, and shall have—hear my prayer!—
Whose education should have been your care:
Telemachus may reach maturity
Deprived of fatherly authority.
Think of your father's peaceable demise
If only you were here to close his eyes.
But me, a girl the day you sailed away,
You'd find a crone if you returned today.

DIDO TO AENEAS (VII)

Heroine of the fourth book of Virgil's *Aeneid*, Dido, or Elissa, had fled her native Tyre following the murder of her husband, Sychaeus, by her brother, Pygmalion, to found with her followers the city of Carthage in North Africa, afterwards the inveterate enemy of republican Rome. A fugitive himself after the fall of Troy, Aeneas, son of Venus and the mortal and now-aged Anchises, arrives at Carthage with a handful of survivors including his old father and his young son, Ascanius, or Iulus. His dalliance with Dido cut short by the divine demands of destiny, Aeneas soon sets forth again for Italy. Deserted, Dido expresses a natural impatience with the claims of the historical imperative before killing herself. An amalgam of all the sirens who sought to detain Odysseus on his way home, she might in Ovid's version be any woman abandoned by any man, like any number of his other heroines. Virgil's queen is a more complex and appealing figure, tragic rather than merely pathetic.

Here is Dido's swan song: when you've read
My last words, Aeneas, I'll be dead.
Thus when her time has come, abject upon
The riverbank laments the silver swan.
I do not have a hope that you'll be moved
By prayers the god of love has disapproved,
But, having lost my honor, all I had,
The waste of a few words seems not so bad.

You mean to leave me here—you cannot stay—
An offshore wind has blown good faith away,
And having cast off our relationship

For Italy—wherever—you take ship,
Indifferent to Carthage and her new
Ramparts to be ruled henceforth by you.
What's done you shun, and seek what's to be done,
And having sought throughout the world and won
One land, start looking for another one.
But when you've found it, who will give you, then,
Her land to be exploited by strange men?
Another love? Another Dido? Yet
Other engagements, which you will forget?
When will you found another Carthage and
Gaze down upon the throngs at your command?

But even if all this is granted, O
Where will you find a wife who loves you so?
For you I burn with a religious flame,
And day and night repeat Aeneas' name,
Despite ingratitude, indifference—
I'd do without you, had I any sense!
I do not hate Aeneas—I deplore
Your faithfulness but only love you more.
Pity me, Venus, I am your son's bride!
Befriend your brother, Love, so, mollified,
Aeneas will come over to your side,
And I who loved him first, as I aver,
May find in him my passion's cause and cure.

But I delude myself with fantasy,
You and your mother never could agree:
Wild animals, or rocks and stones and trees—
You were born of parents such as these,
Or else the sea which, wind-swept even now,

You make haste to sail on anyhow.
But why such haste? The wind is in the East:
The wintry weather's on my side at least!
It's you I'd sooner owe this respite to,
But wind and wave are less unjust than you.

Am I worth dying for, that you should flee
(Deserving death for your iniquity)
From me across the vast tracts of the sea?
What exorbitant aversion, this—
Once rid of me and death would seem like bliss!
The waves will soon be calmed, the winds subside,
And Triton on his sea-blue horses ride;
O, like the winds, relent! You know you could,
If you were not inflexible as wood.
You've felt the fury of the elements,
Yet trust them despite your sad experience.
The sea invites you to embark, but keeps
Many a grisly secret in its deeps.
Liars should not risk their lives at sea,
A place that penalizes perfidy,
Especially slighted love, for from sea spray
The mother of loves was born, or so they say.
Abandoned, I fear to hurt the one who so
Hurt me, and dread the shipwreck of my foe:
If I must hate you, better alive than dead—
You take the blame for my demise instead!

If overtaken by a hurricane—
God forbid!—what thoughts would fill your brain?
First your falsehoods, every single lie,
And me by your deceit condemned to die;

The ghastly specter of your wife should rise,
Betrayed, befouled with blood, before your eyes:
"Begone!" you'd cry, "though anything you do
Will be no more than I deserve, it's true."
Each thunderbolt you'd think is aimed at you.
For the moment let your rage give way
Like the sea's. The ransom you must pay
For your safe passage is this small delay—
If only for the sake of your small son.
Is not my life enough to have undone?
Has he or have your household gods deserved
To drown, whom once you from the flames preserved?
Or don't you take these sacred objects, or
Your father whom you boast that you once bore
On your shoulders, with you anymore?
Lies, all lies! for you did not commence
With me your meretricious influence.
What was your little darling's mother's fate?
To be abandoned by her heartless mate.
The story moved me. Lead me to the pyre:
My guilt is more unbearable than fire.

And now your gods have left you, it appears,
Adrift on sea and land for seven years.
I took you in when cast up on our shore
And offered you my crown, almost before
A proper introduction, what is more.
Would with such favors you had been content,
Then our relations might look innocent!
That fatal day when we, afraid to brave
A shower of rain, took refuge in a cave,
I heard voices—nymphs', I thought, but these

Were no nymphs, but the Eumenides
Setting their seal upon our destinies.
Outraged honor, do your worst! I go
To my dead husband full of shame and woe.
I keep his statue in a marble shrine
Which leafy boughs and fleecy wool entwine.
Four times I heard the voice that I thought dumb
Forever, whisper softly, "Dido, come!"
No, this devoted widow won't delay;
Only my guilty conscience makes me stay.
Forgive my lapse; my glib seducer could
Make my bad behavior almost good.
His mother, Venus—and the child whom he
Cherished—bespoke respectability.
So I went wrong, for the right reasons, yet
Had he kept faith, I'd nothing to regret.

The same old fate that worried me to death
Pursues me now, unto my dying breath.
My husband was cut down before his time;
My brother reaped the profit of that crime.
Leaving my husband's grave and home I go
Into harsh exile, followed by my foe.
From him and the sea escaped I'm driven to
This foreign shore, which I acquired for you.
I built a town, and round it a long wall,
A challenge to my neighbors one and all.
Fights break out, the natives seek to try
The strength of foreign females such as I;
My half-built town I cannot fortify.
I have a thousand suitors; all demand
Why I have offered someone else my hand.

Give me to one of them, don't hesitate!
In such a farce I would cooperate.
Then there's my wicked brother: having shed
My husband's blood, he'd like to see me dead.

Lay down your gods, polluted by your touch:
Impious hands do not please heaven much.
Your idols might prefer incineration
To being rescued for your veneration.
Perhaps you've left me pregnant and a part
Of you is hidden under Dido's heart?
The wretched babe will share its mother's doom,
Condemned by you before it leaves the womb.
Ascanius' little brother dies with me,
Confounded in one common penalty.

You say you're leaving at a god's command?
I wish he had forbidden you to land
Here upon the Carthaginian strand;
Even with such a guide, you long were lost
Upon the savage ocean, tempest-tossed.
Regaining Troy would hardly be worth all
This trouble, as it stood before its fall.
Instead of Troy you seek the site of Rome,
But if you get there it won't be like home.
When you are old you may obtain somehow
The long-sought country that eludes you now.
Forego your crooked ways, accept my whole
Realm, and my brother's treasure, which I stole.
Transplant your Troy to this more promising
City, and rule here as anointed king.
If you feel warlike and your young son cries

For more triumphant martial exercise,
I have an enemy for you to face:
Both war and peace are native to this place.

By your mother, and your brother too,
And by those Trojan gods that go with you,
(May those you rescued of your countrymen
Prosper, and war not trouble them again;
May your young son with length of days be blest
And your old father's bones at last find rest!),
Please spare this house, which you are master of:
What crime can you impute to me but love?
No hostile Grecian town gave birth to me,
None of my kinsmen was your enemy.
If making me your wife would bring you shame,
Call me your hostess or whatever name
You please—if I am yours it's all the same.
The winds and tides off Africa I know,
And when they will or will not let you go.
When the wind sets fair you shall set sail,
Now seaweed holds your stranded ships in jail.
Let me decide the time, you'll leave some day,
And if you asked I would not let you stay.
Your shipmates need some rest, so does your fleet,
Whose overdue repairs are half-complete.
For favors past and present, and what may
Come of our union yet—more time, I pray,
And as the sea abates and passion grows
Routine, perhaps I'll learn to bear my woes.

Otherwise, I'll take my life, you'll see:
You shall not long enjoy your cruelty.

I wish that you could see me as I write,
Clasping your broadsword to my bosom tight,
My teardrops falling on the naked blade
Which soon instead of tears will drip with blood—
Your gift was thoughtful, given my sad fate.
My burial expenses won't be great.
This weapon's not the first to deal a blow;
The wounds of love already pierce me so.
My sister, Anna, my sad confidante,
The last respects to my remains will grant.
Sychaeus' wife I shall not be described
As, when my epitaph is thus inscribed:
"Aeneas furnished her the motive and
The means, but Dido died by her own hand."

LEANDER TO HERO (XVIII)

This and the epistle that follows provide the locus classicus for the story, to which Virgil also alludes in his *Georgics,* without naming the lovers. It has an Alexandrian, indeed novelistic ring. Of the many later versions, notably by Musaeus in the seventh century, the most familiar to English readers is Marlowe's splendid if rather overwrought poem.

Dwelling as they do on opposite sides of the Hellespont, she in European Sestos and he in Asian Abydos, Hero and Leander have few opportunities of meeting. Indeed, how they met in the first place, though described by Marlowe and Musaeus, is a mystery in Ovid. Leander, however, has at least once swum the strait, at night, to visit his beloved, and received a warm welcome.

> I send you greetings I would sooner bring
> In person, were the sea less threatening,
> For if the gods were kind, you'd give a better
> Reception to the writer than his letter.
> But they are not—or why do they frustrate
> My plan to swim across this famous strait?
> The sky looks black as pitch, and you can see
> The wind-swept, barely navigable sea,
> But one foolhardy sailor, to transport
> This tender missive, will today leave port.
> I, too, was more than ready to embark,
> But my departure might excite remark,
> And then our love affair, which I'd concealed
> From my family, would be revealed.
> "Go to my love," I murmured as I wrote,

"In her fair hand she'll take you, happy note;
Perhaps she'll kiss you, nibbling, I hope,
With lips and snow-white teeth the envelope."
My fluent hand committed to the page
The rest of all this whispered persiflage.
I'd rather swim than write, and splash my way
Through the accustomed water any day;
But if more fit to cleave the bounding main,
I've wit enough to make my meaning plain.

All week long—it seems a year or more!—
The sea has never ceased to seethe and roar,
But in that time if once I fell asleep
I hope that I may never brave the deep!
Upon a rock I sit and glumly stare
Toward your side; though flesh does not quite dare,
Love and imagination take me there.
I can discern, or think I can discern,
High on your tower the beacon that you burn.
Three times upon the sandy beach I strip
Naked to attempt the awful trip.
The flood obstructs my youthful undertaking;
Over my head tumescent waves are breaking.
Rudest of winds that blow and bluster, O
Boreas, why persecute me so?
You're scourging me and not the sea, you know!
What savagery could you be guilty of
If you yourself had never been in love?
Cold as you are, you can't deny that you
Once burned with passion for a woman too.
How would you feel, if somebody between
You and your airy bliss should intervene?

Moderate your windy vigor, please!
Aeolus himself commands no stiffer breeze.
A waste of breath! He whoops at my request
And does not lay the windswept sea to rest.
If Daedalus would lend me wings to fly
(Though here his son once tumbled from the sky),
I'd take my chances, could my body brave
The air, which used to skim the wavering wave.

Rebuffed by nature's vast indifference,
I recollect my first experience.
At nightfall, it affects me to recall,
Driven by love, I left my father's hall.
My clothes and fear at once I cast aside
To thrash with flailing arms against the tide.
The moon upon my pathway flickered her
Light, like a helpful fellow traveler.
Then, gazing up, I prayed, "Look kindly on
Me, goddess. Don't forget Endymion,
The thought of whom should tenderly incline
You to indulge this enterprise of mine.
From heaven you came to woo a mortal youth;
The maid I love's a deity in truth.
Not to mention her celestial grace,
None but a goddess has so fair a face.
Compared to you and Venus, she'd place third—
But see for yourself, don't take her at my word.
As you, pale silver, radiant and bright,
Surpass the other stars with your pure light,
My love's the loveliest of womankind—
To doubt this, Cynthia, you must be blind."
These words, or something similar, I said,

Then onward through the bending waves I sped.
Reflected in the water, the full moon
Lit up the silent night as bright as noon.
Not a sound disturbed the stillness save
The splashing of my body through a wave.
Only the halcyons lamented low,
Mourning for something—what, I do not know.
My arms grew weary, but I tried to lift
My head above the waves and thick spindrift.
There was the beacon Hero had ignited!
On that dark shore my goddess was benighted!
Suddenly weary arms grew strong once more;
The water seemed more yielding than before.
The love that warmed my heart sufficed to keep
My limbs from freezing in the frigid deep.
The nearer drew your coastline, and the less
I had to swim, the more my eagerness.
As soon at I got close enough to see,
The sight of you there watching heartened me.
I strove to entertain my mistress by
Aquatics, hoping thus to catch your eye.
I saw your nursemaid trying to restrain
Your dashes to the water's edge—in vain,
For though she held you back she could not save
Your feet from a wetting in the foremost wave.
You welcomed me when I emerged on shore
With hugs and kisses well worth swimming for.
My nakedness with your own robe you cloaked
And dried my hair which salty spray had soaked.
The rest is known to us alone, and night,
And to your tower and to its beacon light,

For it would be as difficult to count
The pleasures of that night as the amount
Of seaweed floating in the Hellespont.
How short the time we had in which to taste
Love's joys! We did not let it go to waste.
Dawn had not banished night when Lucifer
Arose, the morning star, day's harbinger.
We traded hasty kisses greedily,
Sorry the night had passed so speedily,
Till, warned by your nursemaid not to dally more,
I left your tower for the cold seashore.
We parted in tears, and, plunging in anew,
As long as I could I kept my eyes on you.
The champion who set out yesterday
Returning seemed a wreck, a castaway;
The route to you was easy, flat, and still,
But coming back the path was all uphill.

Unhappy when I reached my native land,
I'm more unhappy to remain there, and
Is that so difficult to understand?
Why all this water separating us
Who literally are unanimous?
Single-minded as we are, why not
A single country, like a single thought?
Sestos is yours, Abydos mine—what matter?
I prefer the former, you the latter.
But when the sea is up, I am upset
At how obstreperous a breeze can get.
The dolphins all know about our love affair,
And I'm no stranger to the fish, I dare
Say. Through well-trod waters lies a way

As often traveled as a carriageway.
I chafed at this, the only way across,
But now the wind blows I lament its loss.
Today the stormy straits are white with foam;
In weather like this no ship is safe at home.
I guess the Hellespont looked much the same
When from a drowning girl it took its name
And Helle's death insured its infamy.
With such a record, is there hope for me?
I envy Phrixus' luck, whom safe and sound
The golden ram transported in a bound,
But I should need no ship or magic beast—
If it were possible to swim, at least!
I don't lack skill, just opportunity:
Ship, passenger, and pilot I shall be!
I need no Bear to steer by, large or small:
Love knows no public cynosures at all.
Let others on Andromeda rely,
Or on the Crown or on the Wain nearby
Which glitters coldly in the polar sky!
Perseus', Jove's and Bacchus' loves cast no
Light on the doubtful journey I must go.
There is another light more fixed than theirs,
By which in darkest night love never errs.
With such as guide I might attain the shore
Of Colchis, where the Argo sailed before;
Surpassing youthful Palaemon, or him
A weed once made immortal, shall I swim.
When I through giant waves can hardly drag
My weary limbs as vital forces flag,
I tell myself that soon these aching arms

Will be rewarded with my darling's charms,
And then, refreshed, my body cannot wait,
Keen as a racehorse at the starting gate.

Therefore I follow my loved star, and serve
You, for above all others you deserve
A place in heaven. Still, for now remain
On earth, or lift me to a higher plane.
Though here on earth, you're difficult to find.
The stormy sea reflects my troubled mind,
For even though no ocean separates
Us, I'm embarrassed by these narrow straits.
I wonder whether on some farther shore
A world away, I might not hope in more
Comfort: your nearness scorches me like fire;
My only satisfaction is desire.
You are so near that we can nearly touch—
That little *nearly* frustrates me so much,
Reminding me of Tantalus' pursuit
Of shrinking water and elusive fruit.
Can I be happy only when the weather
Permits us now and then to get together?
Why should I pin my hopes on wind and wave
In light of how perversely they behave?
But either I am braver than I think,
Or careless love will bring me to the brink.
Committed to no vaguely distant date,
My good faith I shall promptly demonstrate.
Some passage through the adverse waves I'll seek,
Although the sea stays rough another week!
Then, if my daring meets with no success,
My death will finish my unhappiness.

I hope my body may be cast ashore
Not too far from my destination, for
Then you'll weep and stroke each stranded limb,
And sigh, perhaps, "I was the death of him!"

No doubt this letter, with its reference
To my untimely fate, may give offense.
Now I lay down my pen. O, please, don't weep;
Join in my prayers to pacify the deep.
A little lull I need to reach your shore,
But once I get there, let the tempest roar!
Yours is the port best suited to my prow,
No harbor suits it better anyhow.
If storms confine me there, I'll gladly stay
With you in dalliance all night and day,
Content and in no haste to swim away.
No more the heartless waves shall I berate,
Or curse the cruel currents of the strait.
Long may the winds detain me, and your fair
Arms, twin arguments to hold me there!
When Boreas permits I'll set to sea,
So keep your beacon burning bright for me,
And nightly let this letter fill my place.
I pray that I may follow it apace.

HERO TO LEANDER (XIX)

In this, one of the few straightforward love letters of the whole collection, Hero waits between hope and fear, the Sestos and Abydos of Ovid's dramatic psychology, for what will prove her lover's last attempt to swim the Hellespont. Like Laodamia (XIII), she does not know that her beloved is, if not already dead, doomed, though her unconscious tells her so in a dream. The third, decisive element in this little tragedy of separation and disappointment, the Hellespont, or more modern Dardanelles— the strait, no more than four miles wide, between Europe and Asia at the entrance to the Sea of Marmora—was named for the maiden Helle, who, unlike her more fortunate or tenacious brother, Phrixus, fell into it from the back of the flying ram whose golden pelt later played a role in the saga of the Argonauts and Medea (VI, XII). Helle's mother, Nephele ("Cloud"), and her cruel stepmother, Leucothea ("White Goddess"), or Ino, figure onomastically with other marine deities in Hero's effusion—a dead letter if there ever was one.

> Come, Leander, so that I, in place
> Of writing, may enjoy you face to face.
> The time of joy deferred seems long to me;
> Excuse me, but I can't love patiently.
> Our love is equal but our strength is not,
> For men are braver, so I've always thought;
> Girls' spirits like their bodies are so weak,
> I'll die if you delay another week.
> But you by hunting and by cultivating
> The soil beguile the tedium of waiting;

You loiter at the forum and the gym
Or train a docile horse by bridling him,
Catch birds with snares or fish by hook and line;
Your evening hours are spent awash in wine.
What else is there for me to do but pine
For love of you; such is my loneliness
That even if I loved a little less . . .
Whereas in fact, my only bliss, I burn
With love which you can never quite return.
Sometimes I whisper in my nurse's ear,
"I wonder what is keeping him, my dear?"
I chide in your own words, or near enough,
The horrid wind that makes the water rough,
And then complain, the waves abating some,
That now you can you just don't want to come,
At which complaint tears overflow my eyes,
Tears my sympathetic old nurse dries.
I look out for your footprints on the strand
As if they would stay printed in the sand.
If someone from Abydos comes I make
Inquiry, beseeching them to take
A letter back. How often I've caressed
Your clothes, left on the beach when you undressed
To swim the Hellespont!
               When in the West
Day dies, and friendlier and kinder night
Brings forth the stars and puts daylight to flight,
Upon the roof we set our beacons out
As signals on your ordinary route,
And then with female handiwork beguile
Our tedious vigil, spinning all the while.

You'll wonder what I talk of all night long?
Nothing but Leander is my song.
I ask my nurse, "Do you suppose he's fled
His father's house, while everyone's abed?
Or does their vigilance fill him with dread?
Has he already stripped, you think, to swim,
With olive oil anointing every limb?"
She barely nods, not meaning to reproach
Our love; her old head shakes at sleep's approach,
She mutters suddenly, "He's launched, alright!
His arms divide the billows left and right."
My work half-finished, I anticipate
That you have got halfway across the strait;
Now I gaze forth, now timidly I pray
For a propitious wind to smooth your way.
I strain for every sound, and if I hear
The noise of someone coming, think, "He's here!"
When thus I've whiled the night away with lies,
Sleep supervenes upon my tired eyes,
And then you sleep with me against your will,
And though you do not want to come, you will.
I dream I see you swimming near at hand,
I seem to feel your arms about me, and
As usual, while helping you to dress,
My body warms your dripping nakedness.
The rest, which modesty forbids my spelling
Out, is shameful only in the telling,
But bliss like this is too good to be true:
When sleep deserts poor Hero, so do you.

If only, eager lovers, face to face
We might in actuality embrace!

How many cold and lonely nights I've passed
With you away! You don't swim nearly fast
Enough, but though the sea's still dangerous
Last night the winds were less obstreperous.
What unfounded fear has made you miss
A golden opportunity like this?
For though another chance may soon occur,
This one was better, coming earlier.
Quickly as the sea is roused to fury,
You can get here quicker if you hurry.
If you were stranded here, you'd not complain:
My arms would shield you from the wind and rain.
Then I should view the tempest with good will
And pray the waters never to be still.
What happened, that you're frightened to attempt
A passage that you once held in contempt?
As I recall, the sea appeared almost
As threatening when you approached our coast
And I cried to you, "Not so bold! beware
Lest your courage end in my despair."
Where's your boldness gone that you behave
So timidly, and why? Where is that brave
Swimmer who used to laugh at wind and wave?
But stay as you are, not as you used to be,
And, cautious, only cross a tranquil sea,
As long as you still love me with the same—
As you put it yourself—"eternal flame."
Contrary winds I am less nervous of
Than of your breezy attitude to love,
And lest you fancy hardly worth the prize
The toil and danger of your enterprise.

Will not a European girl be said
Unworthy of an Asian prince's bed?
I could bear almost anything except
Your wasting time, bamboozled by some kept
Woman, so irresistible, no doubt,
That this new love will drive our old love out.
Better death than suffer such a blow!
I'd die before I let you wrong me so.
I don't say this because you've given me
Any reason for anxiety.
No gossip has alarmed me recently,
But I fear everything—all lovers do,
And absence makes the heart more anxious, too.
Better the misfortune that one knows
Firsthand, than vague misgivings, I suppose.
Imaginary sufferings I feel
In fact at least as poignantly as real.
Please come, but if you can't I hope it's your
Father's opposition stops you, or
The wind, and not the pleading of some whore,
Knowledge of which would bring me to the grave:
So if you want to kill me, misbehave!
You won't; I'm silly to be terrified:
Only bad weather keeps you from my side.
Worse luck! The surf upon the shore beats loud,
The light of day is stifled in a cloud,
A misty cloud that overhangs the water
Like Helle's mother weeping for her daughter,
While her stepmother punishes the same
Body of water for its hated name.
And now this spot seems every maiden's bane;

Here Helle died, and here I live in pain.
But why should Neptune come between us, who
Can boast of his own indiscretions, too?
Unless the tale of Tyro bedded by
Him, or Amymone, is a lie?
And Calyce? and Laodice the fair?
Medusa with no serpents in her hair
Yet, as well as several Pleiades,
And others whom I've read about? For these
Are some of those with whom once Neptune lay
In love—or so at least the poets say.
Then why should such an old Lothario
Obstruct with storms the way you used to go?
Have pity, pitch your battles on the high
Seas, sea lord; we're separated by
Only a little strait, my love and I.
Against great ships you should perform great feats,
Or, feeling more ferocious, sink whole fleets;
Frightening young swimmers seems to be
Unworthy of the ruler of the sea,
Befitting, instead, some pond-divinity.
Well-born, Leander does not claim descent
From Ulysses, whom you so resent.
God help us both! For all my hopes with him,
Depending on his prowess, sink or swim.

My lamp—for I am writing by lamplight—
Gutters, surely an auspicious sight?
Nurse sprinkles the glad flame with wine, and drinks;
Tomorrow we'll have company, she thinks.
Yes, keep me company, and through the foam
Glide here into my heart, your chosen home!

You're absent without leave, return to base!
Alone in bed I take so little space.
Your fears are groundless. Venus loves the brave,
And she for you will smooth her natal wave.
I too like to swim, but then the strait
Did not present such dangers as of late.
Phrixus and his sister crossed the same
Water, yet it bears a woman's name.
You probably are anxious lest you lack
The time, and strength, to get you here and back.
Let's start from different sides and meet halfway
Across, and kiss each other midst the spray,
Then each return to our respective shore—
Better than nothing, this, but not much more.
Either our shame, which makes a secret of
Our love, must perish, or our secret love!
Torn between self-respect and passion, should
I opt for what seems best, or what seems good?
As soon as Jason came to Colchis, he
Bore off Medea with his argosy,
Nor did the Trojan fancy man delay
In carrying his Spartan spoil away;
As soon as you reach me you leave me, though,
Swimming when a vessel cannot go.
Triumphant in your turgid element,
Be bold but never overconfident.
Well-built craft have foundered off these shores—
You think your arms are stouter than their oars?
Sailors dread the swimming you adore,
Though when their ships break up they swim for shore.
For pity's sake ignore these feeble pleas!

Be stronger than my remonstrations, please!
And persevere until, your course complete,
You throw yourself exhausted at my feet.
Yet every time I gaze upon the flood
A nameless apprehension chills my blood.
No less frightened by my dreams last night,
I exorcised it by a magic rite.
My lamp was burning low as dawn drew near,
That time when true dreams usually appear.
The spindle tumbled from my sleepy hand,
I laid my head upon the pillow, and
Thought I saw, as plain as plain could be,
A dolphin splashing through the windswept sea
Till, cast up on the sandy waterside,
His life, poor creature, went out with the tide.
What does it mean? I'm frightened. Don't dismiss
My dream, and risk your life on nights like this.
Consider my peace of mind if not your own,
For my well-being rests on yours alone.
The waves, subsiding, promise calm to come,
And soon you'll find your route less wearysome.
Meanwhile, as you cannot swim the strait,
I hope this letter cheers you while you wait.

ACONTIUS TO CYDIPPE (XX)

Like Hero and Leander, Acontius and Cydippe belong rather to
romance than to myth. Callimachus in his *Aitia,* or *Origins,* says
that he culled the story from a collection of legends of Ceos by one
Xenomedes. But the conventional happy ending adumbrated in
this letter and, more conclusively, the following one mark the
material as more romantic than legendary. The central predica-
ment (and it is that rather than a plot) turns upon two favorite
elements of folklore, a trick and a vow—specifically, a vow elic-
ited by a trick. It is worth noting that in Latin *votum* could mean
both a formal vow and a wish, like *voeu* in French. In the temple
of Diana at Delos the nubile maiden Cydippe, a pilgrim, im-
pulsively picks up an apple which an unknown admirer has rolled
her way and, more imprudently still, reads aloud the improbable
inscription calling Diana to witness that Cydippe would wed no
one but Acontius. Since such enunciation in such a place con-
stituted a solemn vow, it seems unfortunate that for the ancients
reading normally meant reading aloud. Noted neither for placa-
bility nor for her sense of humor, Diana at once heard and ratified
the involuntary engagement. Thereafter each time Cydippe at-
tempted to marry anyone else, she fell sick. An appeal to Apollo's
oracle at Delphi elicited the advice to fulfill the vow made to his
sister. Acontius' follow-up letter, shifty as his responsibility for the
initial subterfuge would suggest, seems hardly designed to endear
himself or gain, as he does, his devious ends.

> Don't be afraid you'll plight your troth anew,
> Once was enough for you to say *I do!*
> Read on, perhaps your malady may be
> Alleviated by my sympathy.

What modesty! You're blushing, I divine,
As you did lately at Diana's shrine.
As your betrothed—no pickup—I demand
Your hand in marriage, not a one-night stand.
Repeat the words you found inscribed that day
Upon the apple that I threw your way—
I trust you still recall your maiden vow
At least as clearly as the goddess now?
My feelings are unchanged, but more intense,
My passion aggravated by suspense;
The length of time and your encouragement
Enflamed a love already violent.
You led me on; my heart was soon misled.
You can't deny it, every word you read
Diana heard; I saw her nod her head.

I grant you could say I deceived you too,
As long as you admit love made me do
It in the hope our hearts might be entwined—
A motive that perhaps will change your mind!
By nature and upbringing I was never
Tricky; it is you who made me clever.
Cunning Love united us with those
Words which I scarcely needed to compose,
Since he himself drew up the marriage deed.
With Love as counsel I was shrewd indeed!
Call what I did a trick, and me a cheat:
Is coveting your heart's desire deceit?
I'm writing to present my case again,
Another trick of which you may complain!
So be it! If by loving I offend,

I'll woo you, let me warn you, to the end.
Some take the girls they like by violence;
Will one well-written letter give offense?
Please god, I mean by other means to bind
Your will and wholly captivate your mind.
I have a thousand wiles; I've just begun,
And in my ardor I'll try every one.
Believe it or not—the outcome's in the gods'
Laps—but you'll be mine against all odds.
You may escape me once, but Love has snares
More than you know to take you unawares.
If cunning fails, I'll try what force can do,
And in my lusty arms I'll kidnap you.
I don't blame Paris, or whoever can
Successfully impersonate a man.
I, too—but, hush! No, losing you would be
Worse than incurring the death penalty
For rape. To be politely wooed you should
Be plainer: such good looks don't make for good
Manners. The fault is yours; your eyes, as bright
As stars, enflamed my carnal appetite.
Your golden hair and ivory neck are such
Allurements! and the hands I love to touch!
Your grace and gait, so modest and refined!
Your feet, which bring a goddess' feet to mind!
I do not doubt the beauty of the rest:
If I could praise it all I would be blest.

Struck by your bearing and your beauty both,
Of course I wished to hear you plight your troth.
What if you are the victim of a plot,

So long as you admit that you are caught?
I've risked your wrath; now where's my recompense?
Is there no prize for such a grave offense?
Rail all you like at me, and be annoyed,
As long as you're not too cross to be enjoyed.
Given an opportunity to please,
The anger that I roused I shall appease;
Just let me gaze into your tearful eyes
And dry them with considerate replies,
Or, like a slave afraid that you will beat
Him, clasp my humble hands about your feet.
So summon me, the law is on your side—
Why should I in absentia be tried?
As might a mistress, call on me at will
And pull my hair and scratch my face, I'll still
Endure it all as long as it entails
No damage to your dainty fingernails.
Don't fetter me in manacles and chains
Whom love for you so slavishly constrains.
Then you yourself will say, when you recover
Your temper, surely, "What a patient lover!"
Yes, when you see what I can take, you'll say,
"Seeing how well he serves me, well he may
Serve me, and love and honor and obey!"
Tried in absentia, my innocence
Cannot be proved, for want of a defense.
My dirty trick was a discourtesy,
Granted, but you've no one to blame but me.
Diana does not merit a rebuff;
Breaking your word to me was bad enough,

For she was there and saw how you blushed red
When tricked, and memorized the words you read.
Now heaven help you! There is nothing worse
Than (God forbid!) that slighted goddess' curse.
For instance, only mother love proved more
Devastating than her savage boar;
And Actaeon she changed into the prey
Of hounds with whom he used to hunt all day;
The goddess turned proud Niobe to stone
To weep for her children, childless and alone.

I shrink from a true diagnosis, lest
You think me biased by self-interest,
Yet I must tell you why you did and will
Always upon your wedding eve fall ill.
The goddess, saving you from perjury,
Preserves both you and your fidelity,
And every time you try to be untrue
To me, she comes between your sin and you.
Don't make the virgin huntress more irate;
She can be kind if you cooperate.
Take care of your beauty; let no fever blight
Frail limbs and features framed for my delight,
The subtle blush that seems to fade and glow
Faintly beneath your skin as white as snow.
As for my unsuccessful rivals, did
They envy me a chronic invalid?
Your marriage and your sickness so distress
Me, really I can't decide which I like less.
I'd hate to think my clever little trick
Had done you any harm or made you sick.

I wish your perjury were on my head!
I'd take my sweetheart's punishment instead.

Anxious to know how are you are doing, I
Would hang about your doorstep on the sly,
Bribing a maid or serving man to tell
How was your appetite? Did you sleep well?
I'm sorry I can't nurse you, stroke your head,
And hold your hands while sitting on your bed;
Sorrier still, that while I am elsewhere
The man I can least tolerate is there,
Beside your sickbed, ministering to you,
Detested by the gods, and by me too.
Taking your pulse, he'll make that a pretext
To squeeze your alabaster arms, and next
Caress your breasts, and maybe steal a kiss—
What kind of payment for a nurse is this?
To whom do you thus prematurely yield?
Who's this trespasser in another's field?
Hands off the body of my fiancée!
Those breasts are mine, each kiss he steals away;
She whom he fondles is my bride-to-be:
Soon he'd be guilty of adultery!
Tell him to find himself another whore:
This article's already spoken for.
If he has doubts, show him the fine print in
Our contract, and he'll see it's genuine.
Away with him! Unless I am mistaken,
He's got no business here: this bed is taken.
Whatever other contract he may name
Is worthless; I have got a better claim.

Your father pledged you to him, that I grant,
But isn't your pledge to me more relevant?
Mere mortals witnessed the paternal oath;
A goddess ratified your plighted troth.
He fears the name of liar, you, of jilt,
But whose, I ask you, is the greater guilt?
See the respective risks you ran, and what
The upshot is: you're sick and he is not.
Also, your rival suitors' motives are
Quite, like their hopes and fears, dissimilar.
He's on safe ground; my suit's a matter of
Life or death, for I already love
What he perhaps may come to love some day.
He'd yield to me, if he observed fair play.

But since the brute refuses me my due,
I write this letter, Cydippe, to you.
He brought on you Diana's curse and your
Sickness; you ought to drive him from your door.
The cruel perils that you undergo!
I wish that he were dead who treats you so!
Reject him—for he is no goddess' choice—
Then you and I will certainly rejoice.
Don't fret, you're going to get better now;
Remember the temple where you swore your vow.
The gods do not delight in slaughtered cows,
But in the sanctity of secret vows.
For health some undergo the surgeon's knife,
And bitter medicines may save a life:
Forget such treatments, merely keep your word,
And we and our engagement are secured.
Your ignorance proclaims you innocent.

The promise that you made by accident
I and your illness painfully remind
You of, in case it ever slips your mind.
If you defy Diana's ban and live,
You'll beg for her assistance when you give
Birth; she will think she's heard that voice before,
And ask who was your child's progenitor.
You'll swear . . . but well she knows you swore in vain:
Forsworn, you may deceive the gods again.

It's not my own displacement by a rival
I take to heart, but Cydippe's survival.
Your parents weep for you, but do not know
The sin for which you are afflicted so.
Why not inform your mother? No disgrace
Attaches to your conduct in this case.
Tell how I first observed you at divine
Service, a virgin at the Virgin's shrine.
Perhaps you even saw me stop and stare,
Transfixed by sudden admiration there?
And saw—one sure sign of infatuation—
Me drop my cloak in open fascination?
I really don't know how it fetched up at
Your feet, inscribed with cunning writing, that
Apple which you picked up, so curious
You read aloud the superscription, thus
In a divinity's sight betrothing us.
Then spell out for your mother, word for word,
The vow you read and which Diana heard.
"Wed him the goddess sent you," your mama
Will say, "Your betrothed will be my son-in-law;
Her candidate is good enough for me."

Now that's what motherly advice should be!
But if she wants to know my name and rank,
She'll find that you have much for which to thank
Diana. Ceos is my island home,
Nymph-haunted, washed by the Aegean's foam;
And if by lineage you are impressed,
No one denies that mine is of the best.
I'm rich, I am respectable; above
All, am I not attached to you by love?
Whatever his character, you can't refuse
The man you'd choose if you were free to choose.

In dreams Diana bade me write to you,
Which Love, when I awoke, suggested too.
His arrows have already pierced my heart;
Look out for her vindictive, fatal dart.
Our fates are joined; for both our sakes relent,
For you alone can cure our discontent.
If you consent, the wedding march will sound,
And blood of sacrifice bestrew the ground.
With these two lines I'll dedicate a votive
Apple of gold, and explicate my motive:
Acontius' apple shows as bold as brass
That what was written on it came to pass.
Now, lest a longer letter weary you,
I'll close with a conventional adieu.

CYDIPPE TO ACONTIUS (XXI)

Whereas Acontius' motives were as straightforward as his methods were underhanded, Cydippe is more difficult to read. Some would say that these two letters, even more than the others, were basically about reading and its fatal consequences; and perhaps this is what moved some monastic scribe in the dark ages to place them last in the collection. Certainly Cydippe goes to lengths of circumlocution extreme even in Ovid to avoid repeating verbatim the formula which its author, Acontius, repeatedly urges her to reiterate; she even, in line 1, tries to read without moving her lips. Throughout her reproachful, but not contradictory account, she dithers, wavers, and finally surrenders, not so much to her importunate and surreptitious suitor as to the persistent literal-mindedness of divinity. Both she and Acontius refer—tit for tat as is the way with such topoi—to the metamorphosed fortunes of Acteon, who for voyeurism was changed into a stag and hunted down by his own hounds, and Niobe, whose boast that her numerous progeny surpassed Latona's twins, Diana and Apollo, was punished by them with the death of her children and her own transformation into a weepy stone.

I read your note in silence, scared to swear
By some old god or other unaware.
Again you might have trapped me, had you not
Already thought me adequately caught.
I shouldn't have read it, only being rude
To you might aggravate the goddess' mood.
Despite my prayers, no matter what I do,
Diana still unfairly favors you;

In point of fact, she's more solicitous
Of you than of her dear Hippolytus.
A virgin should protect my virgin years,
Which she intends to truncate, it appears.
I suffer for no reason I can see;
My suffering defies all remedy.
Imagine how, almost too weak to write,
I on my elbow prop myself upright,
Afraid lest any but my nurse should know
Of our clandestine correspondence; so
Outside my room she sits, to those who keep
Asking how I'm doing, "She's alseep,"
She says, so I can write in privacy.
An excellent excuse—a nap can't be
Protracted beyond credibility.
When someone comes whom she cannot refuse,
She spits, a crude premonitory ruse.
I stop at once and leave the rest undone,
And tuck away the letter I've begun.
Later I shall take it out again
And write until my fingers ache. The pain
It costs me you can see yourself. I'm better
Than you deserve—and so shall be this letter!
For your sake was I often all but lost;
For your deceit I paid—and pay!—the cost.
Is this the price at which you praised my charms?
It's me my fatal fascination harms!
Had I struck you as plain—I wish I had!—
My dereliction would not be so bad.
While flattered by your jealousy, it's my
Advantages I am afflicted by.

You won't give up, nor will my fiancé,
Both sworn to stand in one another's way.
I'm storm-tossed as a ship that can't decide
Direction, pushed by wind and pulled by tide,
And when the day for which my parents wish
Arrives, I suddenly fall feverish,
And just as we are going to celebrate
My wedding, Death comes knocking at the gate.
I blush for fear unconsciously I might
Appear to have deserved the goddess' spite.
One blames it on bad luck, another voice
Declares the gods do not approve my choice.
Don't think that gossip spares you: most suppose
Enchantment is the cause of all my woes.
Their cause is hidden, but my woes are plain;
Yours is the rivalry and mine the pain.
Say, what would not your hate be guilty of
If you are so pernicious when you love?
You hate your love, and what you hate you cherish;
To save me, therefore, you should let me perish.
Either, forgetful of your heart's desire,
You'll let me of this foul disease expire,
Or else Diana does not hear your prayers—
For you she probably no longer cares.
Make up your mind: have you forgotten me?
Can you? Or have you slipped her memory?

Oh, how I wish that I had never set
Foot on Delos, or at least not yet!
The voyage was unlucky, launching our
Ship at such an inauspicious hour:
Did I not put my best foot forward when

I stepped aboard the painted vessel then?
An adverse wind twice nearly turned us back—
"Adverse"? I must be mad! I take that back—
A favorable wind it was, that meant
That wretched expedition to prevent,
To stop me going wrong before I went.
Would it had never changed! But to complain
About the wind's inconstancy is vain.
To Delos, then, I could not wait to go,
Attracted by its reputation, though
I thought the ship I sailed on very slow.
I cursed the lazy oars, and sails too few
And far between to catch what breezes blew.
Mykonos and Andros we had passed
When splendid Delos came in sight at last.
I cried far off, "Must I pursue you while
You glide about the deep, elusive isle?"
I disembarked about the close of day,
When Phoebus puts his crimson team away,
But when once more he led them forth for their
Day's work, my mother bade me comb my hair.
Placing jewels on my fingers and
Brow, she dressed me up with her own hand.
Then we set out to greet the isle's divine
Guardians with frankincense and wine.
But while my mother bloody entrails flings
On altars smoking with burnt offerings,
Into other shrines, where my nursemaid
Led me, through the sacred sites I strayed.
Under the portico I strolled, and eyed
The statues and royal gifts on every side;

I gazed upon the altar built of horn,
The tree by which the sacred twins were born,
And all that Delos has to show as well,
More than I recall or care to tell.
And while I gazed, perhaps you gazed at me,
So vulnerable in my simplicity?
I went back to Diana's temple, sure
No other place on earth was so secure.
Right at my feet an apple rolled, which bore
These words—dear me! once more I nearly swore
The oath you tricked me into once before!
Nurse picked it up, perplexed. "Read this," she said,
And so, great bard, your formula I read
Aloud, and matrimony being named,
I blushed at once bewildered and ashamed.
I cast my eyes down, modestly intent,
Those eyes which were your ruse's instrument.
Well, are you happy? What a name you've made
As a man who can take in a maid!
I didn't face you armed with axe and shield,
Like Penthesilea on the Trojan field,
And nor do you Hippolyta's baldric hold
Ransom, chased with Amazonian gold.
Why gloat at the words put in my mouth? Indeed,
A guileless girl is easy to mislead.
Atalanta lost her victory
By stooping for an apple, just like me—
Would you another Hippomenes be?
Too bad you had to taint your dreams with fraud
Dishonestly, because your childish god
Afflicted you with lusts I do not know.

Persuade me, maybe, but entrap me—no!
But why not woo me with those gifts in which
You are yourself so eligibly rich?
Instead of which, you forced me, like a brute,
Although I might have listened to your suit.

What use to you your verbal contracts now,
Or that Diana overheard my vow?
The soul it is that promises. Since my
Soul did not consent, no more did I,
For that alone adds faith to formulae.
The mind always gives good advice, of course.
Without consent, no oath has binding force.
If willingly I said that I would wed
You, claim the duties of the marriage bed;
However, if I gave my word but not
My heart, a worthless phrase is all you've got.
I never meant the words you made me say,
And that's no way to win a fiancée.
Try fooling other women the same way
And follow up the apple with a letter:
If you despoil the rich, so much the better.
Make every monarch promise you his throne,
Make all the world holds valuable you own;
Your literary efforts get results
Surpassing those of more established cults.

But, having said as much, now I've denied
Myself to you, and you have heard my side,
I must admit I dread Diana still,
Suspecting it is she who makes me ill;
For every time the wedding day draws nigh,

The bride falls sick, and nobody knows why.
Three times as he draws near our household altar
Hymenaeus' footsteps seem to falter,
And as he waves it languidly about
Time and time again his torch goes out.
Usually his hair is drenched with scent,
His saffron mantle looks magnificent,
But seeing all the tears here and distress
In painful contrast with his festive dress,
Aghast the garlands from his head he hurls
And wipes the unguent from his shining curls.
Ashamed to look so gay in front of folk
Who mourn, his face grows ruddy as his cloak.
While, woe is me! I'm racked with fever, and
The weight of the sheets is more than I can stand.
I see my parents weeping by my bier,
A dirge instead of wedding hymns I hear.

Maiden and huntress, spare a hunted maid,
Lend me your brother's salutary aid.
Won't it look bad if he should save me, whom
You on the other hand were swift to doom?
While you were bathing in some shady pool,
Did I dare spy upon you like a fool?
Did I neglect, among so many others',
Your cult? Was there bad blood between our mothers?
Perjured, am I? I did nothing worse
Than knowing how to read this wretched verse.

Now, sir, if love is what you really feel,
Let the hands that hurt me help to heal.
Burn incense. Why should Artemis resent

A situation which she can prevent?
Where there's life, there's hope. Why rob me of
My life, and you of all hope of my love?
Don't fear that he who offered me his name
Would lay a finger on my feeble frame;
Though, when allowed, he sits beside my bed,
He scrupulously respects my maidenhead.
Often I cannot tell what's in his mind;
The reason for his tears is hard to find.
Caressing me halfheartedly, "My own!"
He calls me in a nervous undertone.
Of course he feels what I don't try to hide:
When he arrives I turn on my right side,
Close my eyes, pretend I'm sleeping, and
Without speaking brush away his hand,
And then he sighs heartbrokenly that I
Am angry with him, he does not know why.
No doubt you are delighted by his woe?
I shouldn't be confiding in you so,
I ought to be annoyed with you instead
Because of the trick by which I was misled.
You write you'd like to see this invalid—
Yet at a distance look what harm you did!
Accurately, Acontius, your name
Accentuates how accurate your aim;
Missile-like, your letters from afar
Prevent the healing of that psychic scar.
Why come, if not to view my sad remains,
A splendid tribute to your nerve and brains,
Wasting away, as bloodless and as wan

As that pale fruit you pinned your hopes upon.
Far from glowing subtly rosy-hued
My pallor looks like marble freshly hewed,
Or like a silver goblet that when filled
With icy water glistens as it's chilled.
Seeing me now, you would not recognize
Me, or think me worth your enterprise.
My vow—for fear I keep it—you'd remit,
And hope the goddess had forgotten it;
Perhaps you'd make me swear the opposite
Or send me your apologies instead
Of those professions I've already read?
And yet I'd like to grant you your request
To see your bride before she's laid to rest;
Hard-hearted as you are, you'd beg to get
Me to forgive what I cannot forget.

To Delphi we have sent, you may be sure,
To ask Apollo to prescribe a cure.
He too complains, vague rumor whispers now,
That I have failed to keep a solemn vow,
And what Apollo says this letter spells
Out: that oath of yours was rigged with spells.
You must have written something to compel
The favor of the oracle as well.
Since you control the gods, I can't withstand
Their will, and freely offer you my hand.
I've told my mother of the promise made
Under duress, embarrassed and afraid;
The rest is your responsibility.
It seems already quite unmaidenly

To chat with you on paper brazenly.
But now my feeble fingers cannot hold
The pen, no matter what remains untold.
Unless we get together, you and I,
What's left for me to write except, Good-bye?

SAPPHO TO PHAON (XV)

The only real woman of letters among all those imagined here, Sappho of Lesbos was a legend, no doubt in her own time (seventh century B.C.), and for all time to come, having given a name or names to practices and tastes associated with hers. Though our only evidence for the character and indeed existence of Sappho— her poetry—is fragmentary, it gives a strong impression of a supremely gifted woman, once considered the tenth Muse, very different from the pathetic creature pictured here. A creation and butt of the New Comedy and as such a prime example of male heterosexual revenge, this Sappho has in middle age forsaken her normal pursuits and been forsaken by the gift of song, to fall ridiculously in love with a faithless youth, also fabricated by slander, Phaon. When in despair she throws herself into the sea, one is tempted to call the whole episode, in the spirit of Ovid and his sources, Sappho's Last Fling.

> A single glance at this familiar fine
> Hand will inform you, love, that it is mine—
> Or till you see it signed with Sappho's name
> Have you no clue whence this epistle came?
> Perhaps you ask, why elegiacs while
> I'm more proficient in the lyric style?
> My love would weep, and finds the elegy
> More lacrimose than lyric poetry:
> No lyre my teardrops could accompany.
> As when the east wind fans a field on fire
> And crops are scorched, so I burn with desire.
> The fields of Aetna Phaon haunts: no less

Volcanic are the ardors that oppress
My soul. No song comes when I pluck the strings;
It is the free and easy mind that sings.
Nor do the Lesbian maidens, furthermore,
Satisfy me now as heretofore.
Anactoria I no longer prize,
Nor pallid Cydro; worthless in my eyes
Is Atthis also, whom I used to love,
As well as a hundred other objects of
My guilty lust. Now you alone enjoy
Their common property, you naughty boy!

Your age and looks for dalliance seem fit;
Your face snared me when I set eyes on it.
With lyre and quiver you might be divine
Apollo, or, with horns, the God of Wine.
While Bacchus and Apollo chose sweethearts
Unfamiliar with the lyric arts,
To me the Muses dictate flawless verse.
Already my fame throughout the universe
Sounds louder than my fellow countryman
Alcaeus', though his style is nobler than
Mine; and if grudging nature did not grace
My form with beauty, talent took its place.
Short as I am, I gauge my stature by
My reputation, which stands very high.
Yes, I am dark. Was not Andromeda
Pleasing to Perseus, albeit a
Darky from darkest Ethiopia?
White doves with varicolored birds are bred,
The blackbird and the popinjay may wed,
And if your mistress must appear as fair

As you, you'll never find one anywhere.
But on the page I too seemed beautiful,
One woman whose discourse was never dull.

Lovers of course remember everything,
And I remember when I used to sing
You'd steal a kiss while you were listening
And praise that too. I pleased you every way,
Especially in arduous loveplay.
You liked my lewdness, extraordinary
Moving parts and running commentary,
And then the way we lay, all passion spent,
Afterwards, exhausted but content.
Now, like fresh game, the girls of Sicily
Flock to you. No more Lesbian, I'll be
Sicilian, unless those island matrons and
Maids expel you, vagrant, from their land,
Turning deaf ears to all your sweet talk, for
The lies you tell them you told me before.

Goddess enshrined on the Sicilian height,
Succor your poet—I am yours by right.
Must gross misfortune keep her biased course,
Deterred by neither pity nor remorse?

My tears, before I reached my seventh year,
Were shed upon my father's early bier.
My brother spent his fortune on a whore;
The shame was worse than ruin, what is more.
Impoverished, he took to piracy,
Recouping his shameful loss more shamefully.
He hates me for my good advice, in fact—

So much for frankness and a sister's tact!
As if I'd not enough to fret about,
Caring for my small daughter wears me out.
Then you arrived, the latest of my woes.
My boat is rocked by every wind that blows.
Around my neck disheveled ringlets cling,
But on my fingers not a single ring.
My dress is shabby, no gold ornaments
Gleam in my hair, and no exotic scents.
Why should unhappiness put glad rags on?
The only man worth primping for is gone
Away. My soft heart's too susceptible
To falling in love whenever possible.
Either some law laid down at birth by fate
Prevents my heartline ever running straight,
Or learning corrupts behavior, and my heart
Was softened by the discipline of art.

No wonder your youthful bloom bewitched me, when
Adolescence captivates grown men!
I feared you might be kidnapped by the dawn,
But she already has her own Phaon.
If the all-seeing moon should see you, your
Slumbers could endure forevermore;
And Venus would have raised you to the stars
Had she not thought you might appeal to Mars.
Your age, not quite a youth's, no more a boy's,
Embodies all life's beauty and its joys.
Return to my arms, my pretty! I don't plead
For love but for the right to love, indeed.
My eyes, as I am writing, brim with tears:
See, on this page, so many blots and smears.

Once you'd made up your mind to leave, you might
Have said goodbye, if just to be polite.
You left without a tear, without a kiss.
I did not realize how much I'd miss
You; you took no tender keepsake hence
And left me none save your indifference.
But I made no demands; my sole request,
That you would not forget me, I repressed.
I swear by this eternal love of mine
And by my patron goddesses, the nine
Muses, that when I heard my happiness
Had flown, dry-eyed and mute in my distress,
Tears failed me, I had altogether lost
The power of speech, my heart was gripped by frost,
As unabashed, alert to my despair,
I beat my breast and wailed and tore my hair
Much as a loving mother might have done
Over the lifeless body of her son.
My brother, bloated with malicious glee,
Strode, gloating, up and down in front of me
And sneered, discrediting this love of mine,
"What's she sniveling for? Her brat is fine."
Nonetheless, for passion is no prude,
I displayed before the multitude
My sadly lacerated bosom, nude.

Obsessed as I am, you visit me by night,
Phaon, in dreams more candid than daylight.
I meet you there wherever else you are,
But sleep's delights are too short-lived by far.
Sometimes my heavy head seems to recline
Upon your neck, and sometimes yours on mine;

Those sweet soul kisses I cannot mistake
Which you so sweetly knew to give and take.
I stroke you, saying words that might be true:
Language awakens as my senses do.
I blush to tell you all the rest, but my
Pleasure does not leave me high and dry.
But when the real world reappears at dawn
I grieve to see my dream so quickly gone.
Forthwith to grove and grotto I repair
In hopes of finding consolation there,
For grove and grotto formerly had been
Our pleasures' secret, sympathetic scene.
Witless, with my hair unbound, like one
Berserk, to our old rendezvous I run;
A cavern's rough and rocky roof I see,
Which looked like polished marble once to me.
And here's the grove that used to shade our bed,
Spreading a leafy awning overhead.
But where's the sylvan monarch, my lord too?
The spot looks cheap as dirt ungraced by you.
I recognize the mark our bodies made
Upon the grass, each well-known crumpled blade,
And prostrate on the spot which you lay on,
I soak with tears the once-delightful lawn.
The leafless tress seem to forget the spring
In sympathy, and no birds sweetly sing:
The nightingale, grief-stricken for the son
She immolated, is the only one
Still mourning. "Itys!" Philomela cries
While Sappho her desertion versifies;
The wood is still as midnight otherwise.

A sacred spring there is, so crystalline
That many think it harbors some divine
Being. Water lilies spread their rank
Growth like a grove beside a grassy bank.
There, as my weary body sought repose,
Before my tearful eyes a naiad rose
Who said, "Since unreciprocated love
Consumes you, go and seek the headland of
Leucadia, which gazes on the deep;
It's popularly known as Lovers' Leap.
Deucalion thence leapt into the void
For love of Pyrrha, but was not destroyed.
As soon as Pyrrha's stubborn heart was stirred
And love returned, Deucalion was cured.
Such is the tale of the Leucadian steep,
So hurry, and don't look before you leap."
She vanished, having voiced this sound advice.
I wept a while, then rose as cold as ice.
I'll go and find that cliff, just as she said,
And hope love's frenzy overcomes my dread.
Nothing could be worse than this! Yet dare
I trust my flimsy body to the air?
Sustain me on your wings, soft Love, lest I
Make infamous the waters where I die.
Here I shall hang the lyre that was Apollo's
With underneath a line or two, as follows:
"Her lyre a grateful poet offers to
Apollo: made for me, it's made for you."

Phaon, instead of driving me to this
Calamitous and fatal precipice,
Why not return, and by that kindly act

Become my Phoebus both in form and fact?
Or would you rather be the reason for
My death and, harder than the rocky shore,
Behold my body dashed to bits before
You'd take it in your arms—that body you
Praised as clever, and good-natured too.
Now I could wish that I were eloquent,
But sorrow is a grave impediment
To art; woe makes me less intelligent.
I've lost my ancient verve for poetry;
My lyre lies silent, mute with misery.
Daughters of sea-girt Lesbos, nubile choir
Whose names I sang to my Aeolian lyre,
Whose love made me a byword, Lesbian throng,
Gather no more to listen to my song.
Your quondam pleasures Phaon stole away—
"My Phaon," alas! I was about to say.
But bring him back, and I'll return to you;
He gives me inspiration, saps it too.
Uncouth and cold, his heart is deaf to prayer;
My words are wasted on the mobile air.
Phaon, I wish these wordless winds would blow
You home to me: your coming back, though slow,
Would be the decent thing to do, you know.
While votive offerings bedeck your stern,
Why pain me by postponing your return?
Cast off, for Venus, risen from the sea,
Smooths the sea for lovers; winds will be
Favorable, so cast off instantly.
Captain Cupid at the helm will stand

Trimming the rigging with his tender hand.
But, if you're bent on leaving me behind—
And no pretext for doing so you'll find—
Just write a cruel line to tell me so,
And straightaway to Lovers' Leap I'll go.